David Crookes

Cloud
Computing

In easy steps is an imprint of In Easy Steps Limited
4 Chapel Court · 42 Holly Walk · Leamington Spa
Warwickshire · United Kingdom · CV32 4YS
www.ineasysteps.com

:ontains accurate
ted and the
ered by readers

:ir respective

In Easy Steps Limited supports The Forest Stewardship Council (FSC),
the leading international forest certification organisation. All our titles
that are printed on Greenpeace approved FSC certified paper carry the
FSC logo.

MIX
Paper from
responsible sources
FSC® C020837

Printed and bound in the United Kingdom

ISBN 978-1-84078-532-6

Contents

5   Cloud printing   61

6   Microsoft SkyDrive   67

7   Using Dropbox   81

8   Apple iCloud   97

Audio & Video 153

Playing in the Cloud 165

Security in the Cloud 185

Index 189

1 Introducing cloud computing

Cloud computing may sound like a confusing, abstract idea but it can revolutionize the way you work and play.

Traditional computing

Many of us will have grown up using computers, whether for work or play. A very early memory may have been the use of tape cassettes. Although they were painfully slow, they allowed users to load and save programs and data to and from their computers. If they wanted to share a file, they would either hand over the master tape or make a copy on to another cassette. The more they wanted to share, the more tapes they would have needed.

Over the years, there have been many more ways to store programs and data:

- Those who wanted a faster and more efficient way of working had disk-drives. Whether they were 5.25-inch, 3-inch or 3.5-inch, these floppies were faster and more reliable. Over time, it was possible to buy 3.5-inch disks very cheaply too

- The dawn of hard drives meant being able to access programs and save data without having to resort to floppy disks. Once a program was installed then, for the majority of the time, the disk was not needed

- CD-ROMs, DVD-ROMS and Blu-Rays advanced the optical storage format. When it became possible and cheap enough for home and work computers to write to such formats, that too revolutionized the way we worked. Suddenly, we had portable mass storage

- Iomega Zip Drives and small USB sticks proved popular ways to back-up or port data

All of these methods, however, have meant that users have had to work from machines that have their required software installed or they have needed portable storage media to hand.

Without it, their programs or data are put out of reach.

It is something we came to live with but it had its downsides. Collaboration on projects has been more difficult – if you and a friend wanted to work on a Word document, for example, you would have to save it, pass it over, allow the other to change or add bits and then save and and pass it back.

That situation lasted for decades. But things have changed.

How cloud computing works

Cloud computing takes the emphasis away from local computers. It is less about the machine you use at home or on the move and more about what is happening on computers many miles away.

Instead of having to store information on your PC, smartphone or tablet, your data can be kept remotely. It will then be made available to any device that is capable of reading it.

Typically, most cloud computing is conducted via a web browser but there are other ways, including specially-made apps for computers, tablets and smartphones. These act as access points for cloud services. They also mean that you don't always need to have dedicated software installed on your machines.

The benefit of this is clear: suddenly you are not tied to your own computer. You do not even need to be tied to your own phone. All you need is a way of accessing the data and that be done from any machine.

As you can see, this differs from traditional computing because you do not need portable storage media nor are you relying on how robust or fast your machine is. With cloud computing, you are seeing programs and data being managed and provided as a service over the internet and it opens up many possibilities.

Hot tip

If you have an old laptop, why not turn it into a cloud computing station? As long as it can hook up to the internet, you will be able to comfortably run most cloud services.

9

Google

Docs
Create and share your work online

Upload your files from your desktop: It's easy to get started and it's free!

Access anywhere: Edit and view your docs from any computer or smart phone.

Share your work: Real-time collaboration means work gets done more quickly.

Documents   Spreadsheets   Presentations   Drawings   Forms

TRY IT NOW   New Features   ▶ Watch the videos

Don't forget

Although many cloud services are accessed via a browser, there are often dedicated desktop apps as well.

What you can achieve

Most people have been cloud computing to some degree for years. Web-based email is a prime example of items being stored on a remote computer, ready to be accessed via any internet-enabled machine.

But computing in the cloud has become more sophisticated:

- You do not have to install programs on your own computer in order to be able to use them. You could access a word processor through your browser and save your work to a remote computer. It wouldn't matter which computer you used – as long as you had the right log in details, you could access your document on any computer in the world or make alterations to it on your phone or tablet

- It is possible to remotely store any file. You can open a folder on your computer, phone or tablet and save items into it. This will then sync across all of your devices

- Keeping a diary becomes even easier. No longer do you need to constantly have a single diary to hand. You can make amends on your phone, jot details on your computer and see it all come together as one

- Photographs can be taken and viewed by anyone, anywhere simply by storing them in the cloud. You can do the same with video and audio. Indeed, you can have your entire music library stored remotely. This means no more worrying that you don't have your favorite CD to hand and no more feeling sad when you realize you have forgotten to move a song from your computer to your MP3 player

You can stream movies and games, write down notes and share your files and folders with others. You can access what you want, when you want it on whatever internet-enabled device you want it on, all because files are stored remotely.

Best of all, the companies which provide these services tend to make them run as simply as possible meaning fewer headaches.

You will certainly not find yourself fiddling around with complex installation settings.

Who is offering cloud services?

There are a growing number of companies offering cloud services including some very big names:

- Google

  Google has a host of cloud-based services, offering users a word processor and spreadsheet as well as presentation and drawing tools. It also has a brilliant calendar which you can share with other people. It offers storage too

- Apple

  The maker of the iPhone, iPad, iPod touch and Mac is very much an advocate of cloud computing. Its iCloud service puts your Mail, Contacts, Calendar, storage and even the ability to locate a lost phone at your fingertips

- Microsoft

  You would not expect such a computing giant to be left behind which is why it is offering Windows SkyDrive. This allows the cloud to be used for storing and sharing data. Microsoft also bought the business collaboration and social networking platform, Yammer, which allows workers to share files and knowledge within private networks

And that is just the tip of a very large iceberg. With major cloud-based players such as Dropbox, Evernote and OnLive – a service that lets you stream top games direct to even the most primitive of computers and tablets – you can see how cloud-based computing has a very rosy future.

Don't forget

Many cloud-based services also let you access your files offline.

Hot tip

Download the Google Chrome browser to make good use of Google's cloud services. You can download it from https://www.google.com/chrome.

11

Don't forget

You do not always need a cutting edge computer to make use of cloud services. This is certainly the case with OnLive and Gaikai cloud gaming.

Don't forget

You need not be anxious about cloud computing. Most of us will have been using an example of it for years: web-based email. Hotmail, Gmail and many more store their messages in the cloud.

Beware

Do not upload illegal files to the cloud. This can get you into serious trouble with the law.

The possibilities of the cloud

So how can the cloud work for you? Well let us imagine a typical day for the average user:

1 Wake up to a text message saying you have a meeting at 2pm. Use your phone to add an entry for that time in your calendar. When you get to work later, it will be on your computer's calendar too

2 Reply to some overnight emails and write fresh ones using the details of contacts stored in the cloud

3 Open a cloud storage app on your phone as you travel to work. Make amends to a document and save it

4 Arrive at work. Open the document again, see your changes and make some more alterations. Share it with your boss so he can make amendments too

5 Collaborate on a presentation using Google Docs ahead of your 2pm meeting

6 Go for lunch. Have an idea and make a note of it in Evernote on your phone. Back in the office, open your computer's Evernote app and check other notes

7 Meeting goes badly. Open Spotify and play Things Will Only Get Better from the cloud for free

8 Read some documents on the train home and use a cloud-based print service to ensure they are on your home printer when you get back

9 Relax with your iPad, playing a blockbuster game streamed from OnLive

10 Remember you need to buy some tickets. Set a reminder using the mobile app Remember The Milk. See it when you get back to work on your computer

Wi-Fi and Broadband

To make good use of cloud computing, an internet connection is vital. Most people have broadband at home – certainly anyone reading this book will – but when you are working in the cloud, you will need a good connection outside of the home too. This will maximise your benefit of it.

Wireless internet (Wi-Fi)

There are many Wi-Fi hotspots in towns and cities across the world and the number of them continues to grow:

1. Cafes, restaurants and public places such as libraries often have free Wi-Fi. Ask them for details of how to hook up

2. There are also companies which offer widespread coverage. The Cloud network in the UK, for example, has thousands of hotspots. The advantage of these is that you only need to sign-up once

3. Software is available showing you where the nearest Wi-Fi hotspots are. The free Wi-Fi Finder app by JiWire on the iPhone is a good example of this

Hot tip

To use your laptop or phone with Wi-Fi, go to your Settings menu or Control Panel. Your PC, Mac, tablet or phone will look for Wi-Fi hotspots and prompt you for log in details.

...cont'd

Hot tip

As an alternative to Wi-Fi you could use 3G or 4G connections. It is worth considering a pay-as-you-go data package if you have a tablet computer that can make use of the phone network in your country.

Don't forget

Turn off your Wi-Fi if you do not need it, to save battery life on your laptop, tablet or smartphone.

4. Of course, you can use the data which comes with your phone to access cloud services

5. You can also tether your phone to a computer or tablet device. This will allow you to use your cellphone's data plan

6. Do be careful, however, if your data plan is limited. When you tether a phone, you will be eating into your service data

2 Working with Google

Google offers a brilliant way of working in the cloud, whether you are writing a school or college project or producing a report for work. It allows you to collaborate on word processing documents, spreadsheets and drawings with other people and produce presentations. You can access your work on a phone too.

Hot tip

Google Docs can also be used to create simple HTML webpages. Just go to File>Download As and choose HTML (Zipped). The zip (double-click it after saving) will contain a .html doc as well as supporting files.

Don't forget

Documents sent to you by email can be previewed from within your Gmail account.

Google in the cloud

Google is synonymous with the internet. Its search facilities are used by millions upon millions of people every day. Many of them also use the non-search based apps created by this web giant which include the likes of Gmail and YouTube.

In days gone by, you would have had to buy dedicated software in order to produce a letter or manage your home finances. If you or a family member wanted to create a presentation, again you would have needed to install software on to your machine.

But with Google, you do not have to install anything. All of the software is stored in the cloud. When you need to start a writing project, for example, you only need to log on to Google. Your files are saved in the cloud too so no matter where in the world you are, you can access not only the software but your files.

These can be shared with others. You can even collaborate on a project.

Google offers you the chance to create a:

● Document

● Presentation

● Spreadsheet

● Form

● Drawing

● Table

And you only need to log in once in order to access all of these and so much more.

The benefit of using Google is clear:

● There is no software to install

● You do not need to worry about updating the software

● The apps are accessible via any internet-enabled device

● Your saved items are available anywhere, in the cloud

Signing up to Google

Google operates a one-point sign-in for all of its services so you only need a single Google account in order to gain access:

1. Go to https://docs.google.com/ (if you are on the main Google website, you can also click on Drive in the menu bar at the top of the page)

2. Log in using your email and password

3. You are now able to start creating a piece of work

4. If you do not have a Google account, click Sign In at google.com and then, on the sign-in page, click Sign Up in the top right-hand corner

5. Fill in your name. Create a username and password, input your date of birth, gender and mobile phone number, agree to the terms and conditions and press Next Step

6. You will be asked to create a Google profile. You can add a photo

7. When you have finished, click Get Started and you will be taken to the main Google page

8. Click Drive in the menu bar at the top of the screen

9. Now you will see the Google Drive page

10. We are ready to get started, creating our first documents

Beware

Be careful to choose a secure password. Having a combination of letters and numbers makes it harder for your account to be compromised.

Hot tip

When signing up for Google services, you will be asked for your current email address. Google will send details of any unusual activity taking place with your account to this address.

Create an Account

Your Google Account gives you access to Google Docs and other Google services. If you already have a Google Account, you can sign in here.

Required information for Google account

Your current email address:
e.g. myname@example.com. This will be used to sign-in to your account.

Choose a password:
Minimum of 8 characters in length.   Password strength:

Re-enter password:

☐ Stay signed in
☑ Enable Web History Learn More

Get started with Google Docs

Location: United Kingdom

Birthday:
MM/DD/YYYY (e.g. "4/9/2012")

Word Verification: Type the characters you see in the picture below.

Letters are not case-sensitive

Terms of Service: ☐ I agree to the Google Terms of Service and Privacy Policy

Create a new project

Creating a new project is simple. There are two things you can do:

- Create a project
- Upload a project

Here we look at both methods.

Create Project

1 Click on the Create button to the left of the screen

2 Choose from document, presentation, spreadsheet, form, drawing or table

3 You will be taken direct to that project screen

Upload a Project

1 Click on the Upload symbol to the right of the Create button on the left-hand side of the screen

2 A menu will appear. Click on Settings and choose from one of two options, depending on the type of file you are importing to Google Docs:

- Convert uploaded files to Google Docs format
- Convert text from Uploaded PDF and image files

3 Now click on Files and browse for a file on your desktop. If you are converting a file, this will now take place

Hot tip

If you are using the Google Chrome browser, then you can upload entire folders. The option to do this can be found via the Upload symbol to the right of the Create button.

Files...

Settings ▸

0 KB of 1,024 MB used (0%)

Add storage...

Enable folder upload...

Learn more...

Tip: Drag files directly into your Documents List

Working with Documents

We are going to produce a word processing document:

1 Click Create and choose Documents

2 You will see a blank page with a menu toolbar at the top. Click Untitled Document to rename it and click OK

Rename Document

Enter a new document name:

[OK]   [Cancel]

3 You write your document in the main white box

4 To create a new document, click File and then New

5 Google Docs automatically saves your changes as you go along so you need not worry about losing your work

Hot tip

Want to view a Google document without any messy toolbars? Go to View>Full Screen. Press the Escape key to recall the toolbar.

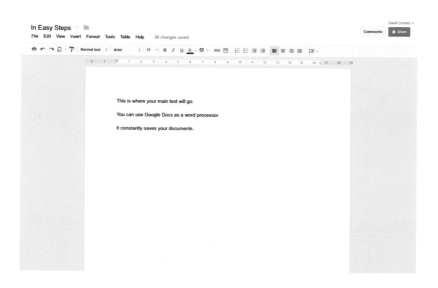

This is where your main text will go.

You can use Google Docs as a word processor.

It constantly saves your documents.

Using format options

As with any word processor worth its salt, you are able to format your text. You can choose the best justification to suit your needs, add bullet points and numbers, change the format and add bold, italics and underline:

1 The toolbar above the main writing area contains most of the format options

| Normal text : | Arial | : | 11 ▼ | B | I | U | A ▼ | 🖉 ▼ | ∞ | 🖼 | ≣ ≣ ≣ ≣ | ≣ ≣ ≣ ≣ | ‡≣ ▼ |

2 The default font is Arial and the default size is 11. Click on these for the drop-down menu to allow changes

3 Click B, I or U for bold, italics or underline

4 Click the underlined A icon to use different text colors. Click the inverted A to change the background colors

5 You can insert links and images via the Link and Image icons in the menu toolbar. You can also click Insert and go to Image or Link

6 You can add bullet points or make numbered lists by using the icon which displays numbers or dots

🖼	Image...	
∞	Link...	⌘K
π²	Equation...	
🖻	Drawing...	
💬	Comment	⌘⌥M
	Footnote	⌘⌥F
Ω	Special characters...	
—	Horizontal line	
	Page number	▶
	Page count	
🗋	Page break	⌘Enter
	Header	
	Footer	
	Bookmark	
	Table of contents	

7 The set of icons to the far right of the toolbar allows you to justify your text left, right, centered or full

8 The final icon will allow you to adjust the line spacing. Click it and you can specify between 1.0 and 2.0

Sharing a document

There is much more to Google Docs than just being able to create your own work and have it available for your own use. You can share your documents and collaborate on them with others:

 Click on File and then Share

 A window will appear. Decide who will have access to your document by clicking Change. You can have:

- Private: only those you list can view

- Public: your document can be viewed by anyone without the need to sign-in

- Anyone with a link: anyone who has the link to your document can view it

If you choose Private, you can add people. Enter their names in the text box on the Sharing settings window. They will be sent an email with instructions

If you choose Public (either via the internet or a link) the link will be displayed in the Sharing Settings window. You can opt to share it via Google+, Gmail, Facebook and Twitter or you can copy and paste it into an email or instant messaging program. Making it public via the internet means anyone can search for your document

In all cases, you can decide on the level of access to your document. Set whether someone can view, edit or comment via the drop-down menu on the Sharing Settings window

Don't forget

As well as sharing, you can also transfer ownership of a document to somebody else. Click the drop-down menu to the right of the name of the person you are transferring to and select 'Is owner'.

Beware

If you decide to transfer ownership of your document (see above), you will not have any control over that file any more so be careful.

Create a presentation

School or work projects can be created with ease when you use Google's Presentation app. Since they are in the cloud, you can work on them and access them wherever you are:

1 Click Create and choose Presentation

2 Choose a theme from the box which appears when creating a new presentation

Choose a theme ✕

Simple Light	Simple Dark	Light Gradient	Dark Gradient
Swiss	Modern	Biz	Khaki
Label	Paper Plane	Spotlight	Traveller

OK   Cancel   ✓ Show for new presentations

3 A template is set up. Click on the words on the first slide to change them

4 To add another slide, click the arrow next to the + icon. You will be given a number of options including:

- Title, Title and Body, Title and Two Columns, Title Only, Caption and Blank

+ ⌄   ↶ ↷ 📋 ⌄ 🖌   ⊡

Title

Title and Body

Title and Two Columns

Title Only

Caption

Blank

5 Again, change or add items to these slides

6 Changes are automatically saved

Don't forget

There are many other templates available to you. You can find lots of them at https://drive.google.com/templates#.templates?type=presentations #.

The Insert Menu

Presentations are so much more than simple text. Using Google's Insert Menu, you can make your presentations shine:

 Click Insert for the drop-down menu. You will see:

- Text Box
- Image
- Link
- Video
- Word Art
- Line
- Shape
- Table
- Animation

2 Choose the type of addition you wish to make by clicking on it

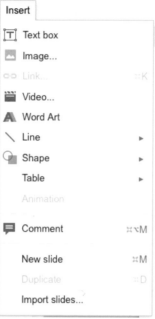

Insert

- ⊤ Text box
- 🖼 Image...
- ⊂⊃ Link...   ⌘K
- 🎬 Video...
- 𝐀 Word Art
- ＼ Line   ▶
- ◔ Shape   ▶
- Table   ▶
- Animation
- 💬 Comment   ⌘⌥M
- New slide   ⌘M
- Duplicate   ⌘D
- Import slides...

Text Box

1 Select Insert and then Text Box

2 Draw a box on one of your slides and size it appropriately

3 Insert text into the box

4 You can highlight the text and change the format of it. Either use the Format menu to add effects such as bold and italics or use the icons in the main toolbar

5 You can resize the box using your mouse by using the squares which are on each corner and side

...cont'd

Image

Don't forget

You can drag and drop an image on to a slide and position it as you would like it.

Hot tip

You can use your webcam to take a snapshot that you can then insert into your presentation.

1 Select Insert and then Image

2 A window will appear. Click Upload. You can drag an image into the main white box or click Upload to browse your hard drive for a picture

3 Clicking URL will let you insert an image via the internet using the picture's unique web address

4 Click Google Image Search to find an image on the web

5 Click Picasa Web Albums if you have images stored using the Picasa service that you wish to use

6 Google also has a stock photography archive which you can access by clicking on Stock Photos

7 Click select and the image will appear in your presentation. Move it around and place it where you want it to be

8 Right-click the image for more options including cut, paste and copy

Insert image   ×

Upload
URL
Google Image Search
Picasa Web Albums
Stock photos

Drag an image here

Or, if you prefer...
Choose an image to upload

Only select images for which you have confirmed that you have a licence for use.   Cancel   Select

Link

 Select Insert and then Link

 A window will appear. Select Web address to insert a URL. You can also link to an email address or a slide

Video

 Select Insert and then Video

 A window appears which lets you search for a video on YouTube. If you know the URL of a video, however, you can insert it by clicking URL

Word Art

 Select Insert and then Word Art

 Type a word into the window which appears and click Enter. It will appear in an art-style font. Clicking on the Font drop-down in the menu toolbar to change it

Hot tip

Change the text size and color of Word Art by selecting it and using the text toolbar options.

Line or Shape

 Select Insert and then either Line or Shape

 Both have extended menus which show you a range of shapes and lines. Choose one and you will be able to place it on your slide. You can resize them with your mouse

Table

 Select Insert and then Table

 A grid appears with circles. Use your cursor to highlight the required number of rows and columns. The table will appear on the slide. You can type into the boxes

Don't forget

A row is horizontal while a column is vertical.

Create an animation

Presentations can be made to look more slick with the addition of animated objects. Any aspect of your presentation can include animation, ranging from fades to zooms:

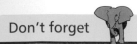
1 Right-click on an element within your presentation and select Animate

2 A menu will appear to the right of the screen. Click on No transition and you will see many options including Fade, Slide from right, Slide from left, Flip, Cube and Gallery

3 Make a choice and then decide the speed from Slow to Medium to Fast

4 Click Apply to all slides

5 You can also choose how an element appears. Click on Fade In and choose from:

- Fade in
- Fade out
- Fly in
- Fly out
- Zoom in
- Zoom out
- Spin

6 Choose whether or not you want it to appear when you click to move the slide on or after the previous or with the previous slide

7 Experiment and then click Play to test

Start a presentation

The beauty of cloud computing is that you could take your Google presentation to a meeting or class and use any computer to open and run it:

Hot tip

The beauty of having a presentation stored in the cloud is that you could just turn up to a meeting and use any web-enabled PC.

1   Log in to your Google account

2   Click on Documents in the toolbar at the top of the screen. Select your presentation from the main Google Docs menu screen

3   Click on Start presentation in the top right-hand corner

4   You can click on the arrow next to start at the current slide or start with speaker notes. The presentation will start, taking up the full screen

Start presentation ▼	Comments

Start at current slide

Start with speaker notes

5   You can use the arrows in the bottom right of your presentation screen to go left or right through your slides

In Easy Steps

27

Create a spreadsheet

For efficient number crunching, little beats a spreadsheet. As with Documents and Presentations, you do not need to have any software installed on your machine in order to use Google's Spreadsheet:

1 Click Create in Google Docs and choose Spreadsheet

2 A spreadsheet will appear. Click on Untitled spreadsheet to rename it

3 You can type numbers into each of the spreadsheet cells. Press tab to move along to the next one or click on a box

4 To save a spreadsheet to your computer, click File and Download as

5 It is possible to save a spreadsheet as:

- CSV
- HTML
- Text
- Excel
- OpenOffice
- PDF

6 Documents are saved to any location you desire on your computer and they can be opened in the relevant app

7 If you prefer to save to the cloud via Google, files save automatically and can be reinstated at any time

Change spreadsheet formats

Different spreadsheets have differing requirements. You can change the format of the numbers you insert into your Google Docs spreadsheet:

Hot tip

If you need to insert a line break, then click on a cell and press Ctrl+Enter.

1   Highlight the cells you wish to format

2   Click on the 123 icon in the main toolbar.

3   There are many choices within this menu from normal through to customized decimals, currencies, time, dates and percentages

4   Make a choice and the format will immediately update

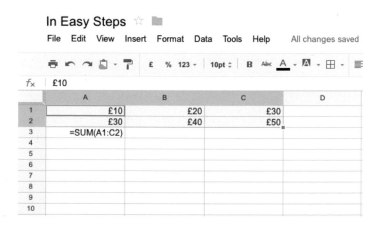

Hot tip

Need to merge a cell?
Select the cells you
want to merge. Click
on the Merge icon in
the toolbar and select
your option. You can
merge all cells or merge
horizontally or vertically.

Add a spreadsheet function

The beauty of a spreadsheet is the ease with which it can make calculations with the greatest of speed:

1 Highlight the cells which you want to include in a calculation by clicking and holding your mouse

2 Click the function icon (the Sigma Σ)

3 Select a function from the list which displays:

- Sum

- Average

- Count

- Max

- Min

4 If the selection of your choice is not there, click More functions. This will take you to a long list of functions. These can be added manually. Ensure all functions have an equals sign before them (=)

5 Click on Show all formulae in order to toggle between the formula and the result

	E		G	
		SUM		
		AVERAGE		
		COUNT		
		MAX		
		MIN		
		More functions...		

Create a chart

A list of numbers on a spreadsheet can cause a headache. One way of sifting through your data is to create a chart based upon it:

1 Highlight the cells you wish to produce a chart from

2 Go to Insert and select Chart

3 A window appears. Your data has been converted into chart form

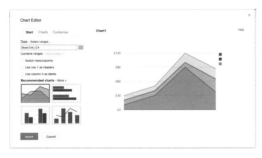

4 Decide if you want to switch the rows and columns the other way around or if you want to use row 1 as headers and column A as labels

5 Click on the Charts tab. You can view other types of charts. Click on one to view how it will look

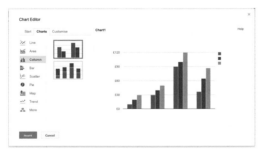

6 Click the Customise tab and include a title, legend and alter the font, axis and columns. Click Insert and the chart will be placed within your spreadsheet

Don't forget

There are many different types of charts. You can choose from line, area, column, bar, scatter, pie, map or trend among others.

Hot tip

Your spreadsheet labels can be used in a chart. Ensure the labels are in Row 1 and Column A of your data and click the boxes next to 'Use 1st row as headers' and 'Use 1st column as labels'.

Create and share a form

If you need to create a question and answer form, Google Docs can again come to the rescue, saving your data to the cloud:

1 Click Create and choose Form

2 You can change the title from Untitled form to one of your choice

3 Fill in some explanatory text

4 You can now type in a question. Include some help text if you want to explain more about the response you are expecting from the recipient

5 Choose the type of answers you wish to receive. You can pick Text, Paragraph text (for longer answers), Multiple choice, Checkboxes, Choose from a list, Scale or a Grid

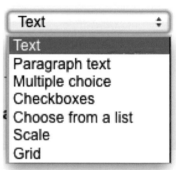

6 Create your answer (or answers depending on the choice you have made)

7 Create another question if you wish. Click Add Item in the top left-hand corner and decide the type of question

32

8　You can also click on Add item to create a page break or section header

Header text	Section title		
Description (optional)			

Done

Hot tip

Questions can be duplicated by clicking the middle duplicate button next to a question.

Share your form

1　Click Share and you will be able to allow others to view your form via Google+

2　You can also click on More actions. This will give you the option of embedding your form in a website or blog. Simply copy the code and paste it in the required position

3　If you look at the bottom of the form screen, you will see a URL. This lets you view your form direct. You can link to this form when you want people to fill it in

In Easy Steps

We are assessing your opinion about this book.
*Required

Would you say the book is..... *
Please choose one option

○ Excellent
○ Very good
○ Good
○ Poor
○ Very Poor

How would you rate the clear instructions?
Please choose from 1 to 5

1　2　3　4　5

○ ○ ○ ○ ○

Submit

Powered by Google Docs

Report Abuse - Terms of Service - Additional Terms

See responses to your form

1　Click on the See responses button at the top of the screen

2　Select summary or spreadsheet depending on how you wish to view the results

Create a drawing

It will not beat Photoshop for flexibility and features but Google's package enables you to work on a drawing, save it to the cloud and open it on any web-connected computer in the world. It can then be inserted into documents, presentations, spreadsheets and web pages:

1 Click Create and choose Drawing

2 The main options are line, text, shapes and inserting images. With these you can produce most drawings

Line

1 Click on the Line icon in the main toolbar or click on the drop-down arrow next to it

2 Selecting the arrow will show you more options. These include: Line, Arrow, Curve, Polyline, Arc and Scribble

3 Make your selection

4 You can now hold down your mouse button in the main drawing area and begin to form your lines

Text

1 Click on the Text icon in the main toolbar

2 Draw a text box. A text-entry box appears. Enter text, using Shift+Enter to create multiple lines

Shapes

1 Click on the Shape icon in the main toolbar or click on the drop-down arrow next to it

2 The drop-down arrow shows you many options. These include:

- Shapes
- Arrows
- Callouts
- Equations

3 Select the one you need. By clicking on each of the options, you will see a range of images that can be placed directly on to the main drawing area

Hot tip

Change the background to your drawing by right-clicking and selecting 'Background'.

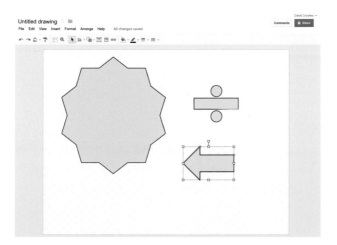

Insert an image

You can also inset an image into the Drawing program. This works in the same way as when inserting an image into a Document, allowing you the same options, and we have covered how to do that in depth in the section entitled The Insert Menu earlier in this chapter.

Hot tip

Importing two or more sets of tables will allow you to merge the data together. Click Merge, select the tables, tell Google which columns you want and give the new table a name.

Hot tip

Clicking Edit will let you modify your data, adding and deleting elements of it.

Creating tables

The tables feature is new. It lets you upload data sets from spreadsheets and visualize it on maps, timelines and charts:

1 Click Create and choose Table

2 You will be asked to import a table either:

- From your computer

- From a Google Spreadsheet

- Or produce an empty table

3 You will be asked to grant permission for the app to access the data and then it will load

4 Specify the columns to import and click Next

5 Give the table a name. Check if you want to allow an export of your table (this will allow others to export the data into CSV format). Attribute the data, give it a description and click Finish

6 The data will be produced as a table

7 Click Visualize to see the data presented in different ways

3 Using Google Drive

Google Drive offers storage facilities in the cloud and it also allows you to collaborate with other people.

Set up Google Drive

Google Drive is a service that allows you to store files online. You can upload and access photographs, videos, documents, PDFs and any work which you create using Google Docs. Your Google Docs files will be saved to Google Drive.

Your uploaded files can be accessed via:

- A PC or Mac
- An iPhone or iPad
- An Android phone or tablet

Google Drive allows you to collaborate with other people on projects. Files can be shared and they can also be edited by others. It is a competitive service too. You are given:

- 5GB of storage space for free
- The ability to upgrade to 25GB or 100 GB for small amounts of money each month
- The option to have as much as 16TB of storage space

Getting started with Google Drive

1 Go to https://drive.google.com/start

2 Click on Sign In

3 Input your usual Google log in email and password. If you do not have one follow the steps on page 17

4 You will see a welcome screen. Click Try Google Drive to get started

Hot tip

Google Drive expands on Google Docs. Fortunately any files that have been created using Google Docs are stored in Drive without taking up any of your 5GB limit.

Don't forget

Search is Google's primary function so it goes without saying that you can easily search through the content of your Drive files.

Download Google Drive

To get the best out of Google Drive, you may want to download the desktop app to your PC or Mac:

1 On the Google Drive website there is a menu on the left-hand side. Click Download Google Drive

2 You will be asked if you agree to the Google Terms of Service. Select Agree and download if you do

3 Google Drive will ask you to run or save the app. Save it to a destination on your hard drive

4 Open the file that downloads and choose to install it. If you are using a Mac, drag Google Drive to your Applications folder

5 Double-click on the Google Drive icon to launch it (or go to Launchpad on your Mac)

6 Google Drive will place an icon in the system tray of a PC. It will put the icon in the menu bar of a Mac computer

7 Sign in to the app using the email and password you use to log into Google Drive

8 A special folder will be created. Files from Google Drive on the web will sync to your Google Drive folder

With Google Drive on your computer, you can quickly access your files and folders. The desktop app treats Google Drive like any other folder on your machine.

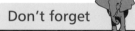

When you make a change to a file on the web, it will be saved to your desktop Drive folder and vice versa. All files and folders are synced.

Upload files to Google Drive

Google Drive allows you to upload files and folders. You can do this via the website or by using the Google Drive app.

Upload via the website

1 Click on the red upload icon which is positioned next to Create and a menu will appear

2 Google Drive is designed to work best with the Google Chrome browser. If you have this installed and are using it, select either file or folder and skip to step 5

3 Some other browsers will require you to install an applet. Select Enable folder upload and click on Install applet

> ×
>
> Enable folder upload
>
> Your browser doesn't support the uploading of entire folders.
>
> If you would like to use this feature, install the Chrome browser (recommended) or the Folder Upload applet.
>
> Learn more
>
> [Download Chrome] [Install applet] [Cancel]

4 The applet will install. You can now click the red upload icon and select Files and Folders

5 A window will appear, allowing you to browse for the required files or folders. Choose the one(s) you want and click Select. They will be uploaded to Google Drive

Upload via the desktop app

1 Click on the Google Drive icon in the system tray of a PC (or menu bar of a Mac)

2 Find a file or folder on your computer and drag it to the Google Drive folder. You can use the Google Drive folder just as you would any other folder on your computer

40

Share your Google Drive files

It is possible to use Google Drive to share your files and folders with other people. Not only that but you will be able to collaborate with others on a project, giving each person with whom you share the file or folder a set level of access:

1 On the Google Drive website, find a file or folder you wish to share

2 Right-click on the folder and select Share. Then select Share again to bring up the Sharing settings box

3 Add the name, email address or group you wish to share with

4 Click Can edit to see the drop-down menu. Select whether you want people to edit, comment or view your file or folder

Send document by email

Hot tip

Sometimes sending a document by email is the easiest method, especially if the recipient is not a very experienced computer user.

Hot tip

The Open document format can be used with many apps including OpenOffice.org, LibreOffice, Scribus and Microsoft Office 2007 and 2010.

As well as giving somebody access to your document online, you can quickly attach it to an email and send it:

1 Open a document. Click File and scroll down to Email as an attachment

2 A window will appear. Choose the format you wish your attachment to be in:

- HTML
- Open document
- PDF
- Rich Text (RTF)
- Plain Text
- Microsoft Word

  You can also choose to paste the document into the body of an email

3 Decide on the recipient of your email

4 Write a Subject and Message

5 Tick the box to send a copy to yourself

6 Click Send

Email as Attachment

Attach as

HTML ▾

To (required) Choose from contacts

Subject
In Easy Steps

Message

☐ Send a copy to myself

Send   Cancel

Save or publish a document

There are times when you do not purely want a document to be saved in the cloud:

 Open a document. Click File and go to Download As

 You can have your work exported in a number of formats:

- ODT
- PDF
- RTF
- Text
- Word
- HTML (Zipped)

  Make your selection

3 You will be prompted to save the document or open it in a program on your computer

Publish to the web

You can publish your document to the internet:

1 Click File and go to Publish to the Web

2 Decide if you want to automatically republish when changes are made to the document

3 Click Start Publishing

4 Your document will be published. You will be given a link to the document that you can type into a web browser. Alternatively, you can use the embed code. Copy and paste the code into a website

5 Click Close

6 Click Send

Don't forget

Although it is convenient to have files stored in the cloud, having a version saved locally is a good back-up, especially when it comes to important files that you want to keep doubly safe.

Set up offline Drive access

Don't forget

You will need to set up offline access to Google Drive for every computer on which you want to use it.

Beware

Don't enable offline access if you are on a public or shared computer otherwise you will compromise your data's security.

Hot tip

You cannot edit Google Doc documents and spreadsheets offline although you can view them. Non-Google Doc files can be viewed and edited.

It is possible to access Google Drive even when you do not have internet access which makes it easy to move folders, view documents and work with any file that is stored in your Drive folder unless it is a Google Doc one:

1 You need to set up offline access using the Google Chrome browser so download and install it if you already have not

2 Go to https://drive.google.com

3 Click on the cog icon drop-down menu and select Set up Docs offline

> Sort ▾
>
> Display Density:
>   Comfortable
>   Cozy
> ✓ Compact
>
>   Temporarily use the classic look
>
>   Settings
>   Upload settings   ▸
>   Manage apps
>   Keyboard shortcuts
>   Help
>
>   Set up Docs offline ^beta

4 In the window which appears, select Allow offline docs

5 Now click Install from Chrome web store to install the Docs Chrome web app, then click Add to Chrome in the Chrome web store and Launch App to complete

> **Set up Docs offline** ^beta   ✕
>
> 1. Allow offline docs (view only)   2. Install the Docs Chrome web app
>
> Recent Google documents and   You need the Google Docs Chrome web
> spreadsheets for   app to manage your offline documents
> davidmarkcrookes@gmail.com will be   and spreadsheets.
> synchronized and saved on this
> computer for viewing only. Learn more
>
> If you're using a public or shared
> computer, don't allow offline docs.
>
> ✓ Step 1 complete   [Install from Chrome web store]

Create a new folder

As well as making alterations to existing files and folders and storing them in the cloud, you can also produce new folders:

 Click on the add folder icon on the Google Drive website

Treat your folders like you would on your computer. It is perfectly possible to have folders within folders.

You will be asked to give the folder a name. Type the name of the folder into the box and and select OK

Rename

Please enter a new name for the item:

New Folder

OK   Cancel

Right-click on your Google Drive icon on your Desktop and select Preferences. You can now choose which folders you want to sync. Just tick the box next to 'Only Sync some folders to this computer'.

If you want to create a new folder using the Desktop app, then click on the Google Drive icon in the system tray of your PC or the menu bar of a Mac

Select the option for New Folder

New Folder

Get Info

View   ▶
Clean Up
Clean Up By   ▶
Arrange By   ▶
Show View Options

The folder will work in the same way as other folders on your computer. You can delete it or rename it by right-clicking and choosing the required option

Google Drive on the go

Hot tip

You can access documents via Google on any web-enabled phone by going to docs. google.com

It is possible to use Google Drive on a smartphone or tablet with apps for Android, the iPhone and iPad available from Google Play and the Apple App Store:

1   Go to Google Play on your Android phone or the App Store for your iPhone and iPad and download the Google Drive app. If you have Google Docs on your Android phone, you will see an option to upgrade

2   The Google Drive apps allow you to browse your online storage space. Tapping on a file will allow you to open it to view its content

3   On an Android phone you can create a document by clicking the document icon next to the magnifying glass. Choose a document or spreadsheet. A document can also be made from a photo or via your phone's gallery

4   You will be asked to give your document a name. Your document will then be viewable no matter which web-enabled device you are using

5   When a file or folder is changed or deleted on a smartphone or tablet, the alteration will also appear on any other Google Drive device including web and desktop and vice versa

4 Google Calendar

With Google Calendar, you can harness the power of the cloud for your day-to-day organization. With the ability to share calendars and invite others to events, you will never again miss a party or appointment.

Set up Google Calendar

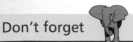

Don't forget

Calendars from other services can be imported. Export your calendar from a package such as iCal, Yahoo or Outlook as an iCal or CSV file, then go to Google Calendar. Go to Settings and, under the Calendars tab, select Import Calendar.

Google Calendar is a free application which allows you to create events, set reminders, see other people's schedules and send invitations. You can share your calendar with friends, family and colleagues too.

Google Calendar is available on smartphones as well as via the web. Any amendments you make will sync across all devices. You can access your calendars on any internet-enabled computer in the world:

1   Go to google.com

2   Log in using your existing Google email address and password. If you do not have one, click on Sign Up to create an account

3   Now click on Calendar at the top of the browser screen. If you can't see it, click on More to find it

4   You will now see the main Google Calendar screen

Google Calendar views

Hot tip

You can use keyboard shortcuts to quickly cycle through the views. Press D for day, W for week and M for month. For custom or agenda views, press X or A.

Hot tip

Highlight dates on the calendar in the left hand column, and the main calendar will show you that selection.

...cont'd

Hot tip

If you want to customize your day view, go to Settings and select Custom View under the General tab. You can choose 2, 3, 4, 5, 6 and 7-day views as well as 2, 3 and 4 weeks.

4 Days view

Don't forget

To refresh your calendar, just tap R.

Agenda view

Add an event

1. Click Create

2. Give the event a title

3. Add a date. You can click on the date to call up a miniature calendar

4. Indicate when your event will start and when it will end

5. Under the Event details tab, input the location of the event

6. Select which Calendar you want to use (you can set up multiple calendars)

7. Write a description

8. You can give your event a color too

9. When you have finished, click Save

Add a Quick Event

1. Click the downward arrow next to Create

2. Type in your event using words, for example: Meeting at airport at 8pm today

3. Click Add and it will be placed on your calendar

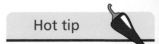
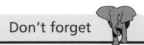
CREATE ▼		Sun 3/25	**Mon 3/26**

Quick Add

Meeting at airport 8pm today

Add

Example: Dinner with Michael 7pm tomorrow

Set a reminder

With Google Calendar, you should never miss an appointment again. The Calendar has an in-built reminder system to alert you to forthcoming events:

1 When you create an event, a reminder will automatically be set. An alarm on a calendar entry shows a reminder has been created

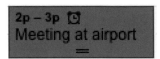

2 By default, it will remind you by both email and pop-up 10 minutes before the event starts. If you have a mobile phone associated with your account, then you can also receive reminders via SMS

3 To alter the period, simply click on it and change

4 Click on the drop-down menus to change minutes into hours, days or weeks if you wish

5 Click on Add a reminder to add more options. You can have multiple reminders set at different intervals

6 If you need to delete a reminder, click on the cross beside the one you do not need

7 When you have finished, click Save

Receive SMS reminders

In order to receive text message reminders on your phone, you have to let Google know your number. You may have inputted this if you have an existing account with Google. If, however, Google is not recognizing your number, then you have to enter it:

Don't forget

You do not have to pay in order to receive SMS reminders from Google.

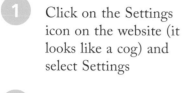 Click on the Settings icon on the website (it looks like a cog) and select Settings

2 Choose the Mobile Setup tab

Hot tip

As a quick way to call up the Settings menu, just press S.

3 Select your country

4 Type in your cellphone number.

5 Click Send Verification Code

6 You will be sent a code to your phone. Enter the verification code on the website and click Finish Setup

7 Now when you create an event, scroll down to the Reminders section

8 Select Add a reminder

9 Use the drop-down menu to select SMS if you wish to receive a reminder on your phone

10 Click Save

Change your notifications

You can manage the way you are reminded about events. This helps to put you in greater control of your diary:

1 Click the drop-down arrow next to your calendar in the list on the left of the Google Calendar screen. Select Notifications

2 You can change the default event reminders. If you want to add SMS as default, for example, click Add a reminder and choose SMS

3 You can also alter the period before each event. Change the number and use the drop-down menus to choose between minutes, hours, days and weeks

4 Google Calendar lets you decide how you would like to be notified. Simply click the tick box next to the options to turn them on or off

5 You can choose whether you want to be notified by Email or SMS for the following:

- New events (for when you are invited to an event)

- Changed events (for when an event is updated by someone else)

- Canceled events (for when an event is canceled)

- Event responses (for when a guest has reponded to an event on your calendar)

- Daily agendas (if you want notifying of your whole day's events – this is sent at 5am daily)

6 When you have finished, click Save

54

Add guests to an event

1 Create a new event or edit an existing one

2 Add an email address in the Add guests box

3 Click Add and your guest will show on the screen

4 You can delete the guest by clicking the cross next to his or her email address

5 Google Calendar lets you decide if guests can:

- Modify an event

- Invite others

- See your guest list

Beware

6 Decide what you want your guests to do by ticking and unticking the boxes

Be absolutely sure that you trust your guests to modify an event when adding them. They will be able to make changes to your calendar entry.

7 You can send an email to your guests. Click Email guests and a window will appear. Type in a message and send it

8 When you have finished, click Save

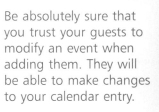

55

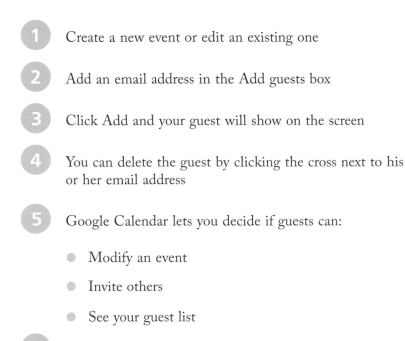

Add guests

| Enter email addresses | **Add** |

Guests can ☐ modify event
☑ invite others
☑ see guest list

Share your calendar

One of the benefits of Google Calendar is the ability to share it. Others can then see what you are doing each day and they can also be given permission to create events for you:

1 Click the drop-down arrow next to your calendar in the list on the left of Google Calendar screen. Select Share this calendar

Display only this Calendar

Calendar settings

Create event on this calendar

Share this Calendar

Notifications

2 Enter the email address of the person you would like to share your calendar with

3 Click on See all event details. You will see a drop-down menu. Choose an option then click Save:

- See all event details lets invitees view your calendar

- Make changes AND manage sharing lets invitees alter events and allow others to share your calendar

- Make changes to events allows the invitee to amend your calendar

- See only free/busy just lets people see if you are available

Share your calendar with non-Google users

Don't forget

Embedding a calendar into your website can produce some wonderful dynamic content.

Not everybody is on Google Calendar and not everyone wants to be. If you need to share your calendar with a non-user, however, the good news is that you can:

1 Click the drop-down arrow next to your calendar in the list on the left of the Google Calendar screen. Select Calendar Settings

2 Under Calendar address, you will see an HTML icon. Click on this

3 A pop-up window will appear showing a URL. Share this URL with others. When they type it into their browser's address bar, they will be able to view your calendar

4 Click OK to finish

Embed your calendar

1 Select Calendar Settings from the drop-down arrow next to your calendar in the left-hand list

2 Look under Calendar address, for the section titled Embed this Calendar

3 You will see some code. You can copy this code and paste it into a website. The calendar will then appear within your blog or webpage

4 Click OK to finish

Add a friend's calendar

If you know a friend has a Google calendar, you can request to share it. Any calendars that have been made public will be instantly made available to you:

Why not add some pre-made calendars? Go to Settings, click the Calendars tab and select Browse Interesting Calendars. You can choose from national holidays, sporting events, stardates and more.

1 In the list on the left of Google Calendar screen, you will see an option which says Other calendars

2 Type the email address of a friend who you know has a calendar in the box entitled Add a friend's calendar

3 If your friend's calendar is public, it will appear in your list of calendars. Otherwise, a pop-up window will appear. It will ask you to send an invite. You can also include your own message

4 When your friend grants you permission, you will be able to view his or her calendar

---

Add a friend's calendar   ✕

Contact Email: info@   [Add]

Enter the email address of another person to view their calendar. Not all of your contacts will have calendar information that is shared with you, but you can invite them to create a Google Calendar account, or share their calendar with you.

Invite Person: **dm@hotmail.com does not have a Google Calendar account**

Type in a brief message to invite this person to Google Calendar.

I've been using Google Calendar to organize my calendar, find interesting events, and share my schedule with friends and family members. I thought you might like to use Google Calendar, too.

[Send Invite]

Print your calendar

1 Click to the right of the Google Calendar screen and select Print

2 A print window will appear. Select your print range

3 Choose your font size

4 Decide if you want portrait or landscape

5 Tick Show events you have declined if you want everything from your calendar to be printed

6 Choose black and white or colour printing

7 Press Print to send it to the printer, or click Save As to save it as a PDF

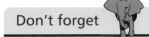

Don't forget

Depending on how big a selection of your calendar you want to print, it may not always fit on the same page.

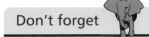

Google Calendar and Android

You can sync your Google Calendar data using Google Sync on the iPhone, BlackBerry, Windows Phone and Android. But since Google created Android, its Calendar service works better on Android handsets:

1 Open the Calendar app on your Android phone

2 Press the Menu button on your phone. Select More and then press New Event to add an entry. Fill in the event name, date and time, location and description. Choose the calendar you want to use, add guests and set a reminder. Tap Done when finished and it will be added to your calendar

Event details

What

| Event name |

From

| Mon, Mar 26, 2012 | 13:50 |

To

| Mon, Mar 26, 2012 | 14:50 |

Time zone

| (GMT+1:00) London, Dublin |

All day ☐

Where

| Event location |

Description

3 Your calendar is automatically synced with the web version of Google Calendar

4 Press the Menu button to call up options for the type of view and to change which calendars you want to see

5 Cloud printing

Make better use of your printer by sending your print jobs to the cloud.

What is cloud printing?

Cloud printing lets you connect your printers to the world wide web. It means you can select to print from any web-connected computer, smartphone or tablet and have it appear on the printer of your choice.

In this section, we are going to look at three popular services:

- Google Cloud Print
- Apple AirPrint
- Printopia

Of these, the first will work with any computer while the final two are optimized for Apple devices.

Having a printer connected to the internet allows you to:

- Access your printer from anywhere in the world
- Print from a phone, tablet, laptop or even someone else's desktop computer
- Share your printer with other people without having to resort to having messy wires between each machine and the printer

Some services require you to have a special printer while others do not but if you are looking for a new printer, it is worth watching out for those that are stamped:

- Google Cloud Print Ready, or
- ePrint or AirPrint

Any printer that accepts an email, however, will also work.

Set up Google Cloud Print

Any printer will work with Google Cloud Print. You simply need to have it connected to a web-enabled computer.

However, Google recommends that you use a Cloud Ready printer. These connect direct to the internet rather than via a computer.

These include Epson Google Cloud Print Ready printers, HP ePrint Printers and the Kodak Hero, Office Hero, ESP C310 and ESP Office 2100 series of printers.

Hot tip

Shop online for the best offers on Cloud Ready printers.

Set up your printer

1 Go to www.google.com/cloudprint and log in to your Google account

2 There are two choices. You can choose to add a classic printer or Cloud Ready printer

3 Clicking on Add Cloud Ready printer will take you to a page that lists specific instructions for your model of printer. Follow these through until your printer has been set up

4 If you are setting up a classic printer, you need to have Google's own browser, Chrome, installed

5 If you have set up a classic printer, open Chrome, click on the wrench icon, select Options, or Preferences on the Mac, click the Under the Hood tab and scroll down to find and click the Sign in to Google Cloud Print button. Click Finish printer registration

6 Your printer has now been set up and you will be ready to print via Google Cloud Print

Using Google Cloud Print

Google Cloud Print works most effectively via the Google Chrome browser which you can download for free from https://www.google.com/chrome.

Print via the Google Chrome browser

1. Click on wrench symbol in the top right-hand corner

2. The print window will appear. From the Destination drop-down menu, select Print with Google Cloud Print

3. Tailor the rest of the settings to suit your use and click Print. A window will open. Select your printer and Print

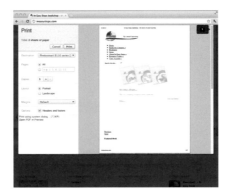

Print via Google Drive on your phone

1. Go to Google Drive at drive.google.com via your phone's browser and sign in to the service

2. Open a document

3. Click on the downward arrow and select Print. Find the printer you wish to use and Print

Using Apple AirPrint

AirPrint allows you to print documents direct from your iPhone, iPod touch or iPad. You need to have an AirPrint-enabled printer in order for it to work. The set-up is quick and automatic:

Don't forget

AirPrint works with many apps including Mail, Photos, Safari, Maps, Notes, iWork, iBooks, PDFs and many more.

1 Open an app which supports AirPrint such as Mail, Photos or the Safari browser

2 When you want to print, tap the Share icon

3 A drop-down window will appear. Select Print

4 Tap Select Printer

5 The app will search for a printer. Make sure your printer is turned on and connected to the web

6 Your printer should appear. Tap its name

7 Tap Print

Using Printopia

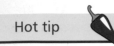

Printopia works on an Apple Mac computer. It allows you to print from an iPhone or iPad to any printer. It does not have to be ePrint or AirPrint enabled. Printopia 2 is free to try but costs a small sum of money to buy:

1. Go to http://www.ecamm.com/mac/printopia/ and select Download Free Demo

2. Install the software on your Mac

3. For Printopia to work, you need to have your Wi-Fi turned on. Your iPad and Mac must have Wi-Fi enabled and they must be on the same network

4. The main interface of Printopia lets you select the printers that can be shared with any device that is AirPrint enabled. This will include Dropbox and Evernote. It will also include Send to Mac

5. Now when you try and print from your iPhone or iPad, you will see that it gives you all of the options which show up within Printopia

6. Select the option you want to print to

7. Now select Print

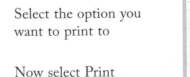

6 Microsoft SkyDrive

With Microsoft's diverse cloud-based application and storage service, it is possible for you to be productive and take your files with you wherever you go. SkyDrive has emerged as a powerful player in the cloud computing market.

What does Microsoft offer?

Windows SkyDrive is a very comprehensive cloud package which brings together Microsoft's brilliant array of apps and services. Anyone who has a Windows Live ID is able to get started straight away.

Here is why you should be using Windows Live SkyDrive:

- You get 7GB of free storage space

- Microsoft Office Web Apps are available. You can create Word, Excel and PowerPoint documents using SkyDrive and these can edited and shared too

- Any notes taken using OneNote on your Windows Phone can be synced with SkyDrive

- The free download Windows Live Mesh lets you sync your computer's folders and files with SkyDrive

- If you alter a document in any way and select save, it will be automatically synced in the cloud

- It works incredibly well with Hotmail, letting you send large files with your emails

- Links can be shared from your Windows SkyDrive space with other users

- You can also use the space to store photos and files that you embed in your blog or webpage

Hot tip

With Windows SkyDrive, you can view attachments in your Hotmail emails.

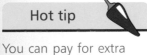

Hot tip

You can pay for extra storage with options ranging from 20GB and 50GB to 100GB.

Microsoft **SkyDrive**

Share documents and work together
Work together and update documents simultaneously using SkyDrive with Microsoft Office.
See how to work together with SkyDrive

sign in

Windows Live ID:

Password:

Can't access your account?

☐ Keep me signed in

Sign in

Don't have a Windows Live ID? **Sign up**
One Windows Live ID gets you into Hotmail, Messenger, Xbox LIVE – and other Microsoft services.

Not your computer?
Get a single use code to sign in with

©2012 Microsoft | Terms | Privacy

Help Centre | Feedback

Opening an account

If you already have a Windows Live ID – that is, if you have a Hotmail account, for example – then you can go straight to https://skydrive.live.com/ and log in with your email address and password. If you do not, there is a Sign-Up option on the website.

Don't forget

You can download and use SkyDrive apps for Windows, Windows Phone, iPhone, iPad and Mac. Go to https://apps.live.com/skydrive for the selection. Simply click the install button for each one you want.

1 Click Sign Up

2 Create a Windows Live ID. You can choose between a Hotmail or Live address

3 Input a password and type in your cellphone number. Give Hotmail an alternative email address. This will be used if there are any problems later down the line

4 Fill in your personal details

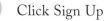

5 Agree to the Terms and Conditions and decide if you want to receive information from Microsoft

6 Your account is now set up

7 Use your email and password to log into SkyDrive

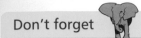

Don't forget

Windows SkyDrive has a filesize limit for web uploads which is set at 300MB.

Hot tip

To upload files of up to 2GB, you can use the SkyDrive apps.

Upload files to SkyDrive

One of the great benefits of Sky Drive is the ability to store up to 7GB in the cloud for free. In order to do this, you need to be logged into your account. We are going to create a folder and then upload files into it:

1 Click on Create folder at the top of the webpage

2 The folder will be created within your My files area and it will allow you to rename it straight away

Create: 🖼 🖼 🖼 🖼 | Add files Create folder View synced folders

Welcome to the new SkyDrive
Finally! Multi-select, right-click, sharing simplified, and over 30 other new features.

My files
David Crookes's SkyDrive

	Name ▴	Date modified	Last modified by
☐	New folder		
☐	Documents	21/08/2010	David Crookes

3 Click on the folder and it will open

4 You now have three options:

- Drag and drop files from a folder on your computer into the main SkyDrive area. The area will turn light blue as you do this

  ◢ Uploading Screen Shot 2012-04-10 at 13.12.27.p ...   Done
  Screen Shot 2012-04-10 at 13.1...   Done
  ☑ Resize photos to 2048 px

- Click Add files from the menu at the top of the screen. Browse your computer for a file that you wish to upload and click Open

- Create a document from scratch. We show you how later in the book

5 Your file will be uploaded to SkyDrive. A window will appear to show the file being uploaded. You will be able to see thumbnails of your images in the main area of SkyDrive

Share your files

Since your files are being stored in the cloud, it makes it easier to share them:

- You can allow others to just view your files

- Or you can let them edit the file as well

Beware

You must have rights to the file or folder you are going to share.

1 Find the file you wish to share in My Files and click it

2 To the right of the screen you will see a panel. One of the options is Sharing. Click it and it will show you an option to Share. Click this. Alternatively, right-click your file and select Share

W	Bargains 3 minutes ago	**View in browser**
		Edit in browser
		Open in Word
		Version history
		Download
		Move
		Copy
		Rename
		Delete
		Embed
		Share
		Properties

Hot tip

Sharing files in this way is much better than constantly emailing each other amendments.

71

3 A window will appear. You can share your file by email, social media or a link

4 If you are sending an email, then fill in the To field and include an (optional) personal message

Send email	Share Bargains.doc	✕
Post to 🅵 🅼 🅻	To:	
Get a link	Include a personal message (optional)	
	☑ Recipients can edit	
	☐ Recipients must sign in to view	
	[Share]	

5 Tick Recipients can edit if you wish them to. Click Share to send it

6 You can work on a shared file at the same time as somebody else. Click Shared in the left-hand column and select the file you wish to work together on

...cont'd

Share via social media

1 If you want to share via social media, you can do so via three defaults:

- Facebook

- MySpace

- Twitter

2 You must sign in to a service however. Click Please connect a service. Choose the social media you wish to connect with and sign in via the pop-up window

3 Click Find more services to add extra social media. SkyDrive works with many websites including Flickr, YouTube, WordPress and Last.fm

4 Use the Search box to find files or folders more quickly. This is handy if you have many items uploaded to Dropbox

Get a link

1 If you would prefer a link, you have three choices:

- A view-only link. This only allows the recipient to see what you are sharing

- A view and edit link. This also allows the recipient to edit what you are sharing

- Make it public. This can be seen by anyone

2 Make your choice via the pop-up Window which appears by clicking Create link

3 Copy the link which appears and paste it into an email program, blog, instant messaging program or anywhere else you wish

Create a document

There are four types of documents which can be created via Windows Live SkyDrive:

- Word
- Excel
- PowerPoint
- OneNote

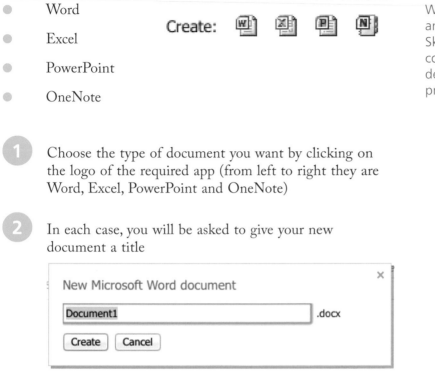

Create:

1 Choose the type of document you want by clicking on the logo of the required app (from left to right they are Word, Excel, PowerPoint and OneNote)

2 In each case, you will be asked to give your new document a title

New Microsoft Word document ✕

Document1 .docx

Create   Cancel

3 Click Create when you have finished and you will be taken to the editing area

Where is my document?

When you go to your main SkyDrive My files area, any documents you have created will appear.

Files are automatically saved and any edits are synced to the cloud. If others are working on your document, their edits will appear within the file stored in your space.

To edit a document, you need to locate it within your SkyDrive space and click on it. SkyDrive will detect which program was used to create it and will open it.

Don't forget

The files you create via Word, Excel, PowerPoint and OneNote on SkyDrive will also be compatible with the desktop versions of those programs on PC or Mac.

Hot tip

With SkyDrive, you have a full office suite and storage space with you wherever you go.

Microsoft Word on SkyDrive

The cloud version of Microsoft Word will be familiar to most people. It is a cut down version of the main package but it still packs a punch with a host of features accessible direct from the on-screen menu. And, if you have it installed, you can quickly open the document in the main Word app.

The interface
Across the top of the screen, you have options to:

- Cut, paste and copy

- Change the font and size

- Add bold and italics

- Underline text

- Justify the text

- Alter the text colour

- Add bullet points

- Spellcheck the text

- Open the doc in Word

Open in Word

The Insert menu

You can insert a table, picture, clip art or a link into your Word document:

1 Click on Insert and choose either Table, Picture, Clip art or Link

2 When choosing Table, select the number of columns and rows you want by scrolling over them. Click to select and insert

3 Choosing Picture will let you browse your hard drive. Clip art will search Microsoft's image library. Link will ask you for a URL. You can then choose the text you wish to see displayed

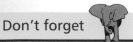

Don't forget

Syncing is automatic so changes made to a document on one platform, be it a computer, tablet or phone, will immediately appear on another.

Hot tip

Your document's formatting is preserved so feel free to add all of the little extras you want from bold to italics and justification.

74

Hot tip

It is possible for one of you to work with the Word web app and Word 2010 on the PC, or Word for Mac 2011 at the same time.

Microsoft Excel on SkyDrive

As with Microsoft Word, there is a cloud version of Microsoft Excel. This spreadsheet app has everything you will need for effective number crunching. Most of the functions will be self-explanatory to anyone who has used a spreadsheet program. The features are similar to those in Google Docs.

The Insert Menu

Click on the Insert menu and you can have some fun with your data by adding charts, functions and tables:

Hot tip

When you collaborate with others on a spreadsheet, changes made by one of you will be instantly seen by the others in your group.

- Function: Add a function to your spreadsheet
- Table: Highlight cells and create a table using the data
- Column: 2D clustered, clustered stack or stacked columns
- Line: Produce lines or stacked lines with markers
- Pie: Choose from a pie or exploded pie
- Bar: 2D clustered, clustered stack or stacked bars
- Area: Display trends of values over time
- Scatter: Gives you various scatter graphs
- Other Charts: Have donut or radar charts
- Hyperlink: Insert a URL and the text to display

The Chart Menu

When you insert a chart, a design tool will appear along the top tabs. These will allow you to make alterations to your chart.

You can add a title for the chart, the axis, the legend and data labels. You can also include gridlines. A chart can be deleted by highlighting it and pressing the delete key.

Microsoft PowerPoint

Don't forget

If you don't like the look of your presentation when you have finished it, you can click Change Theme. All of your content remains intact.

Don't forget

If you want to add a business-like look to your presentation, go to Insert and click SmartArt. This gives you a range of flow diagrams, charts and arrows which give your presentations a lift.

Being able to create a PowerPoint presentation wherever you have a web connection is a powerful thing. Being able to then save it into the cloud to be picked up on any other machine makes this an incredibly valuable tool:

1 Select a theme and Apply

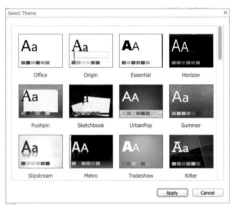

2 Alter any text by clicking on it and rewriting or deleting

3 Click Add New Slide

4 Slides can be duplicated using Duplicate Slide

5 You can insert pictures, clip art, SmartArt and links

View a previous version

Made a mistake? Need to go back to a previous version? Want to see where something went wrong? Windows SkyDrive saves previous versions of your work so you can easily roll back:

Hot tip

The previous 25 versions can be viewed so you should have no trouble finding where and when changes were made.

1 Whether you are using Word, Excel or PowerPoint, you are able to view a previous version of your work

2 Click File and scroll down to Previous Versions

3 The document will open

4 In the main window, you will see the current version of your document. To the left, there will be options to view older versions if any are available

5 Click on any of the Older Versions and they will show in the main window. You can then read through the document to see if you wish to keep it

6 If you would like to revert to a previous version, click Restore Download

Download or print work

There are times when you want a copy of a file you are working on to be stored locally on your own hard drive. With Windows Live SkyDrive, you can do just that:

1 Open a document, whether Word, Excel or PowerPoint

2 Click on File

3 Scroll down to Download a copy

4 A window will appear asking you where on your hard drive you would like to store the document

5 Make your choice and save the document

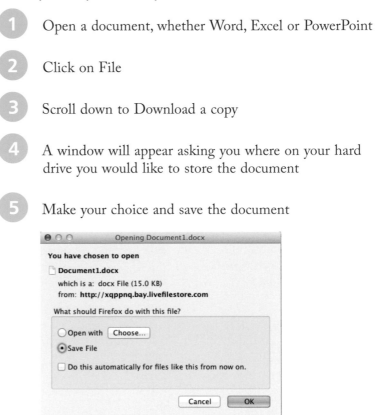

Print

1 You can also print your work

2 Click on File

3 Scroll down to Print

4 In Word and PowerPoint, the file will open in a PDF reader and you need to print from there

5 In Excel, a print-friendly view will show and you can select Print

Hot tip

A PDF viewer is needed when printing via the web apps in SkyDrive so make sure you have one installed. Go to http://get.adobe.com/reader/.

SkyDrive on your mobile

It is all well and good being able to store items in the cloud when you are using a computer but nothing beats the portability of having access to your files on a smartphone. Thankfully there are mobile versions of Windows SkyDrive:

1 On any smartphone, you can use your browser to access Windows SkyDrive by going to skydrive.com

2 But there are also dedicated apps for:

- Windows Phone
- Apple iPhone

3 The apps allow you to add a photo or video and create a folder. You can also send a link. On the iPhone, click on the Share option to see these features. On Windows Phones click the + button

4 Clicking on a file whether you are using the web or phone app versions will allow you to view its content

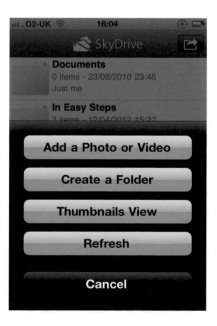

Don't forget

If two people are working on the same document at the same time, a copy will be made. You will be able to view both versions

Hot tip

Have an Android phone? Go to the web browser on your phone and visit SkyDrive.com. Log in when prompted.

Move, copy and delete files

Windows SkyDrive also lets you manage your files, letting you produce duplicates and move them to other folders. You can also delete unwanted files:

 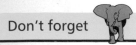
1 In your Windows SkyDrive main area, right-click on an item which you want to manipulate

2 A drop-down menu will appear. Choose to:

- Open
- Move
- Rename
- Delete
- Embed
- Share

My files
David Crookes's SkyDrive

☐ **Name ▴**

☑ 📄 Do   **Open**
☐ 📄 In   Move
☐ 📊 Bo   Rename
☐ 📄 No   Delete
☐ 📊 Pre   Embed
☐ 📊 Pre   Share
☐ 📊 Presentation3

3 Clicking rename will allow you to change the title of a document. Just type into the box

4 If you want to move a file to another folder, select Move. A list of folders will appear. Click on the one you wish to move your file to

The selected file will be moved to:

▲ 🖥 David Crookes's SkyDrive
   📁 Documents
   📁 In Easy Steps

The selected file will be shared with: Just me

[Move] [Cancel]   [New folder]

5 If you want to move a file to another folder, select Move. A list of folders will appear. Click on the one you wish to move your file to. You can also click New Folder

6 To delete a file, click on Delete when right-clicking on a file. You will be asked to confirm if you want to permanently delete the file

7 Using Dropbox

Sync any of your files, regardless of the program you're using, across any computer, smartphone and tablet device using Dropbox – a system that looks like a standard computer folder but has many more useful tricks up its sleeve.

Why use Dropbox?

Dropbox is an amazing service that can be used for free. You get 2GB of storage as standard (with the option of paying if you want more). Best of all? There are no restrictions on what you can upload to your space.

When you install Dropbox on your computer, it acts like any other folder on your PC or Mac. A small, permanent logo is placed on your desktop. Clicking on it opens your Dropbox folder. You can then move files back and forth just as you would between normal folders.

But why is it essential?

- Dropbox can be installed on your computer, phone and iPad
- You can also access your Dropbox folder via the web on any internet-enabled machine in the world
- Files can be opened from your Dropbox folder and any amendments you make will be saved without having to re-upload it
- Files saved to a Dropbox account will also be automatically saved to any device on which you have Dropbox installed
- By placing a file in your Dropbox Public folder, you can share it with others
- People can be invited to share your Dropbox folders
- Dropbox is a great back-up service. Should your PC or Mac fail, you could reinstall your vital files
- A one-month history is kept of your work, letting you go back to fix mistakes and rescue any deleted files
- Dropbox files can be accessed even when you are offline

Smartphones and tablets

There are apps available for the iPhone, iPad, Android, and BlackBerry which allow you to access your files and folders wherever you go. Photos and videos can be uploaded and you can view, share and edit files.

How much does it cost?

Although you can try Dropbox for free and take advantage of the 2GB of storage that it offers as standard, you may find that you exceed this limit. In that case, you may want to pay for extra storage.

There are two main packages to choose from:

- Pro 50

- Pro 100

These offer you different storage amounts:

- Pro 50 gives you 50 GB of storage and it costs $9.99 per month. You can pay $99 for the year which is cheaper

- Pro 100 gives you 100 GB of storage and it costs $19.99 per month. Like the Pro 50, there is a yearly option. It costs $199 per year and is again cheaper than paying monthly

There is also another option: Teams.

This is not aimed at consumers. A Teams account - which gives you 1TB of storage space - lets groups of people share documents, slides and presentations. It costs from $795 for five users.

(Note, all prices correct at the time of printing.)

Businesses will find this much more useful than consumers and it is used primarily for projects which need collaboration between five or more people.

How to choose

The package you decide to use very much depends on your needs. If you are only going to use Dropbox to share and back-up documents, you may find 2GB is more than enough.

But if you are sharing and storing photo galleries, PDFs and other large files and you feel your collection will grow, then you should buy the extra space as and when you need it, starting with Pro 50 before progressing to the maximim limit allowed of 100GB. This top tier will be more than enough for even the heaviest of consumer users.

Signing up to Dropbox

Once you have decided to use Dropbox, the next step is to sign up. You do this via the service's website. The process takes very little time and you will be given an option to download and install Dropbox on your PC or Mac:

1 Go to the Dropbox website at www.dropbox.com on your PC or Mac

2 Click on the 'Sign-in' option in the top right of the screen

3 Do not type in a username or password. Instead click on Create an account

4 Insert your first name, last name, email and password. Tick the box if you agree to the Dropbox Terms and Conditions

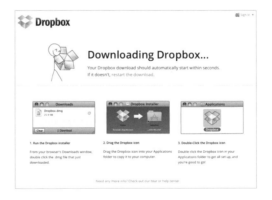

5 Dropbox will start to download its application to your PC or Mac

6 Allow Dropbox to install on your machine

7 Dropbox is now ready for you to use

Installing and using Dropbox

As well as being able to access Dropbox via a web browser, you can also install Dropbox to your PC or Mac.

Dropbox will place an icon in the system tray of a Windows or Linux PC. It will put this icon in the menu bar of a Mac computer, as you can see from this image (the Dropbox icon is to the far left).

Hot tip

When you click on the Dropbox icon, you can see how much space you have and how much space has been used.

When you click on the Dropbox icon, you will see a list of options.

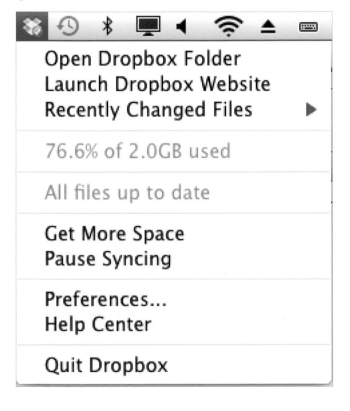

...cont'd

Click on Open Dropbox Folder. The Dropbox folder will open. It will look like any other folder on your computer. The only difference is that the Dropbox folder will show all of the files and folders uploaded to your Dropbox space.

You can use this folder in the same way that you would use any folder. Simply drag a file to your Dropbox folder and it will be copied to your Dropbox space.

Launch Dropbox Website

A second option which is presented to you when you click the Dropbox icon is Launch Dropbox Website. Clicking on this will launch Dropbox in a web browser window and it will automatically sign you in.

Using Dropbox online

You can access Dropbox on any computer across the world as long as it has internet access:

1 Go to www.dropbox.com and log in using your username and password

2 Your files and folders appear in the main part of the screen

3 Clicking on a filename will allow you to open it using whatever software you have on your system. For example, you could open a .doc file using Microsoft Word

4 Use the Search box to find files or folders more quickly. This is handy if you have many items uploaded to Dropbox

Hot tip

Being able to access your files from any internet-enabled computer in the world means you do not need to carry your documents with you on a USB stick.

Upload a file via an internet browser

1 Upload files by clicking on the Upload icon. This is positioned at the top right of the screen. In our image, it is the icon furthest to the left

🔍 Search Dropbox

2 A window will appear. Select Choose Files

3 Select a file (you can choose more than one at a time) and click Open. The file will upload. Select Done to close the window

Share your Dropbox files

One of the handiest features of Dropbox is the ability to share links to files with other users. You can even share them with non-Dropbox users, making it a very versatile system.

Placing items in your Public folder

In order to allow someone else access to your folders and files, you must place them in the Public folder within your Dropbox space:

1. Drag and drop a file into the Public folder within the Dropbox application (see Moving files to the Public folder via the web for browser-based instructions)

2. No matter if you are using the installed application version of Dropbox on your PC or Mac or the web version, open up the Public folder, find the file you want to share and right-click

3. Select Dropbox from the menu and then choose Copy Public Link if using the application. The Copy Public Link option shows up immediately on the web version

4 You can now paste the link into an email and send it

5 When your recipient clicks on the link, he or she will be given the opportunity to download and open your file

6 To remove a file and prevent it from being linked to in future, simply move it out of the Public folder

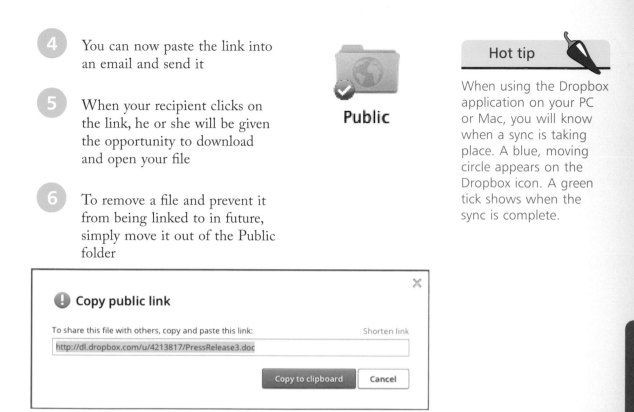

When using the Dropbox application on your PC or Mac, you will know when a sync is taking place. A blue, moving circle appears on the Dropbox icon. A green tick shows when the sync is complete.

Moving files to the Public folder via the web

1 Right-click on a file

2 You will see an option to Move. Select it

3 A Browse box will appear. Search for the Public folder and click. The file will move

Share a folder with others

As well as individual files, it is also possible to share entire folders within Dropbox. This means you can collaborate on projects. Everyone can be given access to the same folder, even if they are accessing it via computers on the other side of the world. Changes made by an individual will be available for everyone to see.

Sharing via the Dropbox application

1. Open up your Dropbox folder on your PC or Mac

2. Right-click on the folder that you wish to share

3. Select Dropbox from the Menu and then choose Share This Folder

4 A window will open into which you can insert the email addresses of the people you wish to share the folder with

---

Share 'House' with others ✕

Invite collaborators to this folder   f Invite Facebook friends

[   ]

(Optional) Send a personal message with your invitation

Enter a message

[Share folder] [Cancel]

---

5 When you click on Share folder, an email will be sent to the people you want to share the folder with. When they click on the link in the email, they will be able to access the folder

Sharing a folder with others via the website

1 Log in at dropbox.com

2 Click on the Sharing option from the left-hand menu

3 Select the New Shared Folder button

4 You can create a new folder or decide to share an existing one. Just make the choice in the pop-up window

5 Select or create the folder you wish to share and add collaborators. They will be sent an email inviting them to gain access to the folder you are sharing

Hot tip

Have you been invited to share a folder? Did you know you can invite others to share folders you've been asked to collaborate on?

Hot tip

You will know when a folder is shared because an image consisting of three people will be embedded on the icon.

Create a photo gallery

Dropbox makes it easy to store images. It even gives you a special Photos folder in which to store them. From here, you can share and organize your pictures:

Hot tip

You can also create a photo gallery via the Dropbox website. Select New Folder when in the Photos Folder and upload images into it. You can also share folders via the website.

Beware

It is not possible to create a Photo Gallery in a private or shared folder. This means that all of the images you put in a Photo Gallery have to be made public.

1 Drag your images into the Photos folder via the Dropbox application on your PC or Mac

2 You can have all of your images in this folder but you may want to create sub-folders within Photos for better organization of your files

3 Right-click (or control-click if using a Mac) on the folder you wish to share. Select Dropbox and Copy Public Gallery Link

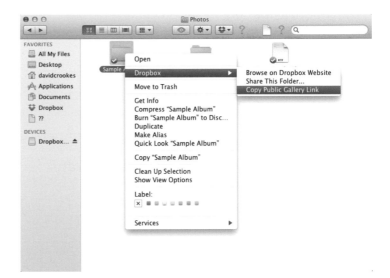

4 This will copy a URL which can then be pasted in an email and sent to friends and family. When they click on the link, they will be able to view your images

Recover your files

If you are working on a file within your Dropbox folder and you make a mess of it, it is possible to recover a previous version. Dropbox keeps copies of any changes you have made to your documents for 30 days. So you can be rest assured that if you have deleted a crucial element, you should be able to get it back:

 1 Right-click (control-click on a Mac) on the file you wish to recover

If two people are working on the same document at the same time, a copy will be made. You will be able to view both versions.

2 Select Dropbox from the drop-down menu and then click on View Previous Versions

> **Browse on Dropbox Website**
> **View Previous Versions**

3 Dropbox will open a web browser. This will show any previous amendments made to your file

4 Click the button next to the version you wish to reinstate. Then click on Restore and it will allow you to see the previous version

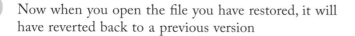

Changed	Event
13 secs ago (current)	🖉 Edited
⦿ 3/10/2012 5:47 PM (oldest)	⊕ Added

5 Now when you open the file you have restored, it will have reverted back to a previous version

Using Dropbox on the go

You can also use Dropbox on a smartphone, allowing you to take your files with you. There are Dropbox apps for the iPhone and for Android and BlackBerry phones. You can also use it on the iPad.

Apple iPhone

Don't forget

Anything you upload or amend on one device can be viewed on another. So if you delete a Dropbox file on your phone, you will not be able to see it on your computer either.

1 Go to the App Store and search for Dropbox. Install it

2 Now open the app and log in. You will instantly see all of the files that are in your Dropbox folder

	O2-UK 🔊	09:54	🔒 🔋

Dropbox Edit

P

PressRelease1.doc
17.0KB, modified 7 months ago

PressRelease2.doc
20.0KB, modified 6 months ago

preview.mp3
3.7MB, modified 7 months ago

Profile copy.zip
195KB, modified 9 months ago

ProtectyourA...one copy.doc
39.5KB, modified 7 months ago

PSM3_2011_04.pdf
62.8MB, modified 1 year ago

Public

Dropbox   Favorites   Uploads   Settings

3 Dropbox will allow you to view most files, from .doc to .PDF. Just tap on the file you want to view

4 Clicking on Uploads on the app will show you the most recently uploaded files

5 When you open a file, you can tap the Star icon at the bottom of the screen. This will add it to your favorites. The icon which looks like a paperclip will let you email a link to your file

Android

 Download the Dropbox app from Google Play on your Android handset

2 Input your log in details

3 The Dropbox app will show all of your files and folders

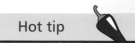
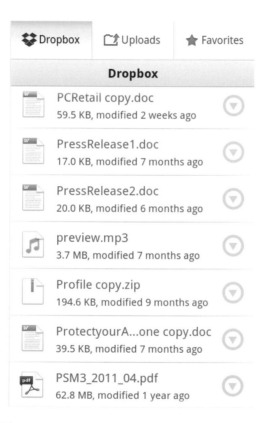

| ✪ Dropbox | ☐↑ Uploads | ★ Favorites |

Dropbox

PCRetail copy.doc
59.5 KB, modified 2 weeks ago ▼

PressRelease1.doc
17.0 KB, modified 7 months ago ▼

PressRelease2.doc
20.0 KB, modified 6 months ago ▼

preview.mp3
3.7 MB, modified 7 months ago ▼

Profile copy.zip
194.6 KB, modified 9 months ago ▼

ProtectyourA...one copy.doc
39.5 KB, modified 7 months ago ▼

PSM3_2011_04.pdf
62.8 MB, modified 1 year ago ▼

4 Tapping Uploads lets you see your more recent files. Tapping on the downward arrow gives you options to share, make favorite or delete a file. You can also Rename or Export a file

5 Press the Menu button on your phone and you will be able to create a New Text File or New Folder. These will sync to your Dropbox account

...cont'd

Don't forget

If you cannot open a file via the Dropbox app, find an app which can. On iPhone or iPad, tap the icon that shows an arrow exiting a box. On Android, tap the blue arrow and select More>Export. BlackBerrys automatically search for the right app.

Hot tip

You can passcode-protect your Dropbox files. You can do this via the Settings option for iPhone and iPad and the Menu button for Android.

BlackBerry

1   Go to https://www.dropbox.com/blackberry/download and choose your BlackBerry device from the list

2   Download and install Dropbox then reboot your phone

3   On the home screen, you need to press the Menu button and go to Downloads. Here you will see the Dropbox icon. Tap it and enter your Dropbox account details

4   Clicking on one of the files or folders will open it. You can also create and share files and folders

5   By pressing the BlackBerry menu button on a highlighted file or folder, you can select from many options including Share this file and Upload a photo. This also offers you Search facilities

Apple iPad

1   Go to the App Store, search for Dropbox and install

2   Open it and log in. You will see your Dropbox files in a drop-down menu to the left of the screen

3   You can open a file by tapping on it. Pressing the Star button will add it to your Favorites. See your favorites by going to Dropbox's homepage, calling up the Dropbox menu and selecting Favorites

4   Articles open within the app but if you have Pages or another program capable of reading your file, click the Open icon and select the required app

5   The paperclip icon will let you email a link or copy it to the Clipboard

8 Apple iCloud

Using iCloud on your Apple devices and computers, you can ensure your vital information is synced. You will also never lose your iPhone again.

What is Apple iCloud?

Making good use of the iCloud means you will have essential files and entertainment with you all the time.

The iCloud service is specially geared towards Apple users. It works on all of Apple's devices – the iPad, iPhone, iPod touch and the Mac – and it seamlessly syncs a wealth of data, storing it all on remote hard drives, ready to be accessed.

With iOS 5 installed on your iPhone, iPad or iPod touch and with OS X Lion or Mountain Lion on your Mac, you are fully equipped to start using iCloud. It comes built-in and ready to use with these operating systems.

You can also use iCloud to help your find your friends and your phone in case it becomes lost.

Apple's iCloud lets you store:

- Music

- Movies

- Photos

- Apps

- Books

- TV shows

- Documents

- Mail

- Contacts

- Calendar

- And much more

Don't forget

Apple says cloud computing will form a major part of its thinking in the years ahead.

98

And in order to effectively store all of this, you get 5GB of free storage space. If this is not enough, however, you can pay extra for more storage with options for:

- 10GB of extra storage

- 20GB of extra storage

- 50GB of extra storage

Set up iCloud on iOS

You can set up iCloud on your Apple iPhone, iPod touch and iPad. If necessary, upgrade your operating system to iOS 5 by plugging your device into your computer and following the prompts within iTunes:

1. Tap the Settings app on your phone

2. Scroll down until you see iCloud. Tap it

3. You can sign in to iCloud using your Apple ID. If you do not have one, you are able to create a free Apple ID

4. You are now signed up for iCloud and you can begin to customize the way you want it to work. When tapping Settings and selecting iCloud, you will see a host of on/off switches

5. Turn off the services you do not want to sync to the cloud and keep those you wish to sync on

6. You will see an option for Storage and Backup. Tap to see how much storage you have and how much has been used. When turned on, the camera roll, accounts, documents and settings automatically back up

Hot tip

If you want your music, apps and books to automatically download, tap Settings, select Store and turn on automatic downloads for the features you want.

99

Hot tip

Do you need to free up space on your phone? When you delete previously bought apps, you can re-download them for free at a later time so do not worry about losing purchases.

Hot tip

To access your iCloud email, contacts and calendars, you will need Outlook 2007 or 2010. To access bookmarks, you need Safari 5.1.1 or Internet Explorer 8 or later.

Set up iCloud on computers

Apple's iCloud can be set up on both a PC and Mac.

Apple Mac

1 Ensure you have OS X Lion or Mountain Lion if you do not already have it

2 Click the Apple icon (in the top left-hand corner) and go to System Preferences

3 Click on iCloud. It will ask for your Apple ID. Enter it

4 It will ask if you want to use iCloud for contacts, calendars and bookmarks and if you want to enable Find My Mac. Make your choice and click Next

5 You will now see the various services which can be saved to the cloud. Tick the ones you want and leave the ones you do not. Close the window

PC

1 You need Windows Vista Service Pack 2 or Windows 7 and later for iCloud. Install the iCloud Control Panel by going to http://support.apple.com/kb/DL1455

2 Click Start, go to Control Panel, then Network and Internet and then iCloud. Enter your Apple ID. You will see the various services which can be saved to the cloud. Tick the ones you want and leave those you do not

3 Click Apply to finish

Find My iPhone

If you lose your iPhone, iPad, iPod touch or Mac, you can use iCloud to discover its location as long as it is connected to Wi-Fi or is on an active mobile data connection:

Don't forget

Many people who have suffered the theft of their Apple devices have managed to locate them using this service.

1 Ensure the Find option is enabled on your iPhone, iPad, iPod touch or Mac:

- On your iPhone, iPad and iPod touch, go to Settings, then iCloud and ensure Find My iPhone is turned on

- On a Mac, click the Apple icon (top left), go to System Preferences, choose iCloud and tick the box next to Find My Mac

2 Download the Find My iPhone app for your iPhone, iPod touch or iPad from the App Store. It is free

3 If you lose your iPhone, iPod touch, iPad or Mac, you can locate them on any PC or Mac by going to https://www.icloud.com/

4 Sign in with your Apple ID and password

5 Click on Find My iPhone

6 Your enabled devices will be listed and located. Click on the device you wish to find and it will be displayed on a map, pinpointing its location

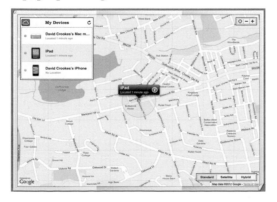

...cont'd

7 Click on the i symbol next to your device on the map

8 A window will appear. You have three options:

- Play Sound or Send Message: This will either play a noise that will help you find the device if it is near by (or alert a robber to the fact you know it has been stolen) or send a message. You could send a message asking for the device to be returned, for instance

- Remote lock: This will prevent access to your device, rendering it useless

- Remote wipe: This will wipe your device of its data, ensuring it does not get into the wrong hands

9 You can also use the Find My iPhone app to discover the location of one of your devices

10 Open the app and your devices will show. Click the device you wish to track and press the blue arrow next to it

11 Decide if you want to Play Sound or Send Message, Remote Lock or Remote Wipe. You can also view it on a map

Contacts, iCal and Mail

By switching on iCloud storage for Contacts, iCal and Mail, you can sync your contact, calendar and email information across the web and your Apple devices. Anything you have stored on one will, if enabled, be viewable on another. You can edit them too:

Hot tip

Sometimes you may struggle to access iCloud via a web browser. Always ensure you have the latest browser and clear your cache. In most cases, this will work.

1 Go to Settings and iCloud on a iOS device or click the top-left Apple icon, select System Preferences and then iCloud on a Mac. Ensure you have Contacts, Calendar and Mail switched on

2 Now when you add to your contacts list or make entries in the calendar apps on your iOS devices or Mac, they will be stored in the cloud

3 By going to icloud.com, you can click on the large icons for Contacts and Calendar. This lets you view them on any web-enabled computer too

4 To use Mail with iCloud, you need a @me.com address

5 Go to Settings via iOS or the System Preferences on a Mac and select the iCloud settings

6 Ensure Mail is turned on

7 It will ask you to create a @me.com account if you do not already have one. Simply input an email name of your choice. You cannot change it once you have done it

iWork and the cloud

If you have Pages, Keynote or Numbers on your iOS device, you can store your documents in the cloud:

Beware

There used to be a service at iWork.com but this was discontinued in 2012. Any work on there cannot now be accessed.

1 Go to Settings on your iOS device and select Pages. Switch on Use iCloud

2 Go back to Settings on your iOS device and select iCloud. Ensure you have Documents & Data turned on

3 When you produce a piece of work within Pages, Keynote or Numbers, your documents will automatically feed into the cloud

Beware

Unless a document has been opened on an iOS device, it cannot be downloaded from icloud.com.

4 You can view your documents on any Mac or PC by going to icloud.com/iwork

5 Click on a document and you can download it. A Pages doc, for instance, will download to Pages '09 or Word. You could also see it displayed as a PDF

6 Click the right-hand cog icon to delete or duplicate documents. You could also upload a document using this method. Select the Upload option

Apps and iBooks

You can sync your apps and iBooks across all of your Apple devices. Not only does this mean you pay just the once but it also eliminates the hassle of having to install separately:

 Tap on your Settings icon

2 Go to Store

3 Turn on automatic downloads for Apps and Books

4 Now when you purchase or install a free app or book on one device, it will be automatically available on another

5 Apple's iCloud will also make a note of your highlights, notes and bookmarks within iBooks as well as your past app downloads and purchase history

Hot tip

When purchasing an iBook on your iPad or iPhone, it will appear – within a very short space of time – on other Apple devices you own.

Hot tip

As well as iBooks, you may want to consider downloading the Amazon Kindle app for PC, Mac, phones and tablets. It works in a similar way, syncing purchases across all devices that you own.

Photos and iCloud

Don't forget

New photos are stored in iCloud for 30 days and they are automatically stored on your computer.

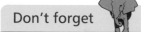

Don't forget

Your last 1,000 photos are stored in the cloud.

When you take a photograph using an iOS device, he it an iPhone or an iPad, you can have it pushed automatically to iCloud. It will then be made available via the Photos app of an iOS device and in a PhotoStream album on a Mac:

1 Tap on the Settings icon on an iOS device. Tap PhotoStream and turn it on

2 On a Mac, click the Apple icon, select System Preferences and ensure PhotoStream is enabled. This will allow it to work with iPhoto and Aperture

3 Take a photograph on an iPad or iPhone and it will automatically be sent to the cloud

4 You can also upload images to iPhoto and Aperture on a Mac. Any images within PhotoStream are imported into your photo library on a Mac where they can be edited, deleted and shared with others

9 Making notes

See something you like and make a note. Keep an eye on websites, create lists, record audio and take snapshots. Then place all of this in the cloud for later reference.

Beware

With Evernote, you have a maximum limit of 100,000 notes (each of which can be 25MB in size for free users).

Don't forget

While Evernote is free, there is a Premium version that adds extra bandwidth and priority support among others (http://evernote.com/premium/).

Hot tip

Want to deactivate your Evernote account? Go to Settings and select Deactivate Account.

Using the cloud for notes

We all need to jot things down. Whether we are making a shopping list, noting a web address or rcminding ourselves of something that we need to do at a later date, instinct often tells us to at least grab a pen and paper.

But you can make notes on your computer or phone. And if you use a cloud-based notemaker, those jottings can be viewed in a multitude of places. Your data is kept on a remote server and it is synced to any device that can handle your notes. Since the vast majority of notemakers will have a web-based version, that means any machine with an internet connection and browser.

Evernote is a popular notemaking application which can be used for Mac and Windows PCs as well as through the Safari, Chrome and Firefox web browsers. It can also be used on the Apple iPhone, Android, BlackBerry and Windows Phone 7 handsets.

Create an Evernote account

1 To sign up using a computer, go to the Evernote website at www.evernote.com

2 In the top right-hand corner of the website, it will say Create account. Click on this

3 Fill in your email address, username and password

4 You will be sent an email with a confirmation code. Enter this on the website and your account will be set up

Create an Evernote Account

Evernote helps you remember everything across all the computers, phones and tablets you use.

Capture anything
Save your ideas, tasks, projects, files, research, and more.

Access anywhere
Evernote makes all of your memories available anywhere you go.

Find everything fast
Search by keyword, tag, and even find text inside images.

Create an Account   or Sign in

Email address

Username

Password

Enter the numbers below

88797

By clicking register your are agreeing to our Terms of Service and confirming that you are at least 13 years old.

Register

Creating notebooks

Notebooks allow you to organize your notes into categories and it is good practice to set one up before starting to create notes. You could have different notebooks for shopping, work and hobbies, for example. We are going to go through the steps of creating a notebook in Evernote via a browser:

Hot tip

On the web, you can move a note between notebooks by dragging it from one to another. Make sure a note's notebook is not being displayed, however.

1 On the left-hand side of the screen, you will see the heading Notebooks and a drop-down arrow. Click on the arrow for the option New Notebook. Click on this

EVERNOTE

▼ **Notebooks**　　　　▼ | **View Options ▼**

New Notebook...

▦ All Notes (4)

1/10/13 Great gene

2 Give your notebook a name. We are going to choose Shopping for ours

New Notebook

Name: Shopping|

Save | Cancel

3 Click on Save and your new notebook will appear in your Notebook list

Create a new note

We are going to create a simple note in Evernote via a web browser:

1 Click on New Note

2 Select a title for your note

3 Choose the notebook in which you want your note to appear. You can learn how to set up a notebook on the opposite page

4 Write your note. You will see that you also have a lot of formatting tools at your disposal such as bold and italics

5 When you have finished, click Done

Done   Auto Save

Supermarket list

Shopping   Set URL...   Show Details

B *I* U x₂ x² ABC — ☰ ☰ ∞ □ 2 @ A ▾ Font Family ▾ Font Size ▾

Eggs
Milk
Bread
Potatoes
Pasta

Share an Evernote note

Sticking with the browser-based Evernote, we are going to look at how you can share a note with others:

1 Look through your Evernote notebooks and find a note you wish to share. Highlight it

2 At the top of the screen, you will see a link called Share. Click on this to see your options

Hot tip

Need to stop sharing a note? Then on the web version click the Shared link below a note and select Stop sharing. You can right-click the note on the Mac or Windows desktop app and select the same option.

3 You can share your note via Facebook, Twitter, or email. Simply highlight the option you want. It will ask you to sign in to Facebook or Twitter. For emails, your email client will open

4 It is also possible to share a note with non-Evernote users by creating a direct URL to it. Select Link

5 You will be shown a URL which you can paste into an email or into an instant messenger client. When the recipient clicks on it, they will be taken to your note without having to sign in or register with Evernote

6 You can click on Shared within your entry and select Stop Sharing if you decide you do not want anyone else to see what you have made a note of

Using Evernote Web Clipper

When you are surfing the web either for research or for fun, you will come across many items of interest. Using Evernote's Web Clipper, you can save those items for later reference.

Download Evernote Web Clipper

1　Go to evernote.com/about/trunk/items/evernote-clippers and click on Get Started. This will detect which method of installation is required

2　You will be directed to Evernote's homepage. Click Get the Web Clipper

Clipping an article

1　To save an entire web article, press the Evernote icon when you are on the website. Select Clip article

2　Evernote will pull the article and send it to your account. When you next log in to your Evernote account, no matter what the platform, you will be able to view it

Clipping full page

1　If you select Clip full page, Evernote will pull the entire webpage into your account. You will be able to see the page exactly as it appeared online

2　Now when you go to your Evernote account that full page will be there

Clip URL

1 Finally, it is possible to clip a URL. This will let you click on the web address at a later time and see the article you have clipped via an internet browser

2 Click on the elephant-head toolbar button and select Clip URL

3 The screen will go black and the URL will show in white. Evernote will then make an entry in your account with the URL for later reference

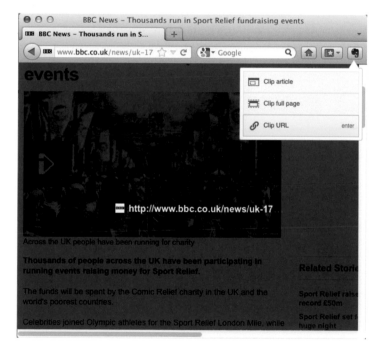

113

Hot tip

Clipping a web page to Evernote captures the URL and the name of the page.

4 As with any Evernote entry, you can delete, print, share or edit your entry so that it works the way you want it

Install Evernote apps

As well as working via a browser, you can download a dedicated app for your PC or Mac. Installing the app means you do not have to log in via a browser and you can take advantage of a slicker interface.

Download Evernote Desktop for Windows PC

1 Go to evernote.com/about/download/ and click Windows on the right-hand menu

2 A setup executable file will download. Save it to your computer and then double-click to launch it

3 When complete, click Finish. You will find Evernote in the All Programs menu. Click on the icon to launch

Download Evernote Desktop for Mac

1 Evernote is available from the Mac App Store as well as from evernote.com/about/download/

2 Search for it in the Mac App Store and install it for free. Alternatively, download the dmg file via the URL in Step 1 and click to install

3 Evernote will be placed in your Applications folder. You can view this via Launchpad in your Dock

Download Evernote Desktop for mobile

You can install Evernote on smartphones and tablets:

● For iPhone, iPad and iPod touch, go to the App Store

● For Android, go to Google Play

● For BlackBerry, go BlackBerry App World

● For Windows Phone 7, go to the Windows Phone Marketplace

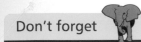

Don't forget

The computer apps offer greater functionality and a bespoke design from the Evernote team.

Don't forget

Mac users see a card view of their notes with more information on them. There is also a word and character count available.

114

Hot tip

Whatever you send to Evernote on the web or via a desktop app will be available on your phone and vice versa.

Recording audio

You can use Evernote to record audio messages that you can store as a note:

 1 Click Audio Note on the Mac or click New Note>New Audio Note on the PC

2 Select Record and start speaking into your microphone. Press Save when you are finished

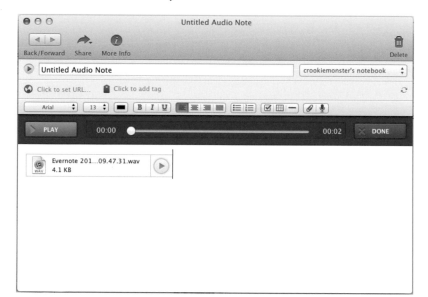

3 Your audio will appear with a playback function. Select Done if you are happy

4 Give your note a title

5 You could share your message by email, Facebook or Twitter or grab a URL of it. Just click the Share option and make your selection

6 Close the window and your message will be saved

Don't forget

Audio can also be recorded on a mobile phone via the smartphone apps. Select the Voice option for iPhone, New Note for Android and iPad (tap the microphone) and Audio Note for BlackBerry handsets.

Hot tip

If your note is otherwise empty, you can record up to two hours of audio. Premium users can record up to four.

Exploring the Desktop apps

The Desktop apps offer the same facilities as the web version with the advantage of not clogging up a browser window.

Apple Mac

The Apple Mac version of Evernote takes on the look and feel of a OS X app and it is easy to navigate the user interface. You can also use your webcam or microphone to take a photo or record audio notes.

116

Use your
webcam

Your
account and
your shared
notes

Sync will
refresh
Evernote

Create a
new note

Record
audio

Search
your
notes

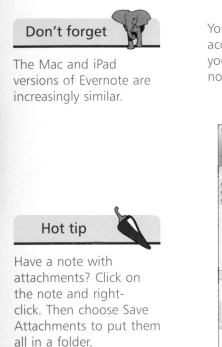

Your
notes

Write
your note

Windows PC

The Windows PC version of Evernote has a simple and yet effective interface which is similar to the Apple Mac. As well as text notes, you can also record audio or video.

Don't forget

If you run Linux there is, as yet, no Evernote version available and it appears unlikely an official one will surface.

Your account and your shared notes

Sync will refresh Evernote

Create a new text, audio or webcam note

Print a note

Your notes

Read your note

117

Exploring mobile apps

The advantage of cloud computing is that you can create and read your notes wherever you are, using smartphone and tablet apps.

Apple iPhone

The Apple iPhone version of Evernote is feature packed. It lets you create notes, use images from your camera roll and incorporate snapshots and audio.

Hot tip

Notes created on the iPhone can make use of your GPS coordinates. Tap Details on a note to see the location.

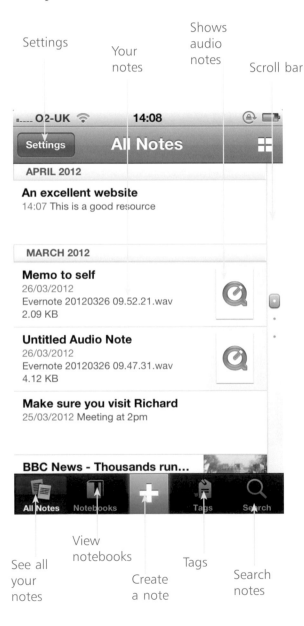

Settings

Your notes

Shows audio notes

Scroll bar

See all your notes

View notebooks

Create a note

Tags

Search notes

When you click on the + symbol, you will be able to create a note. There are many options which allow you to tailor the note for your specific needs and add various attachments

When you have finished, you simply tap Save.

Add styles
such as
bold
Attach
snapshot,
photo or
audio
Attach
an item
Shows
notepad, tag
and location
information
Save note

119

Write your
note here
Subject of
note
Show
keyboard

...cont'd

Clip a webpage via your Android browser by going to the URL you want, tapping the URL and holding then clicking Share. Tap Evernote and create a note before saving it.

Android

The clear layout of the Android version of Evernote ensures that note taking and syncing to the cloud is made easy.

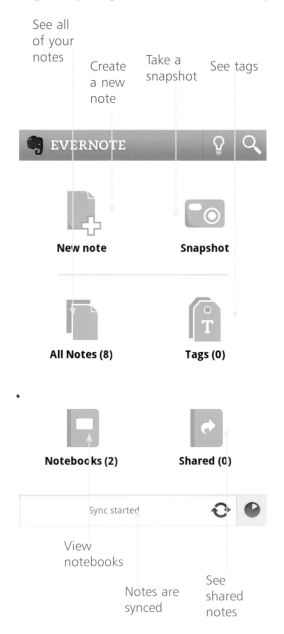

See all of your notes

Create a new note

Take a snapshot

See tags

View notebooks

Notes are synced

See shared notes

Subject and location

Scroll this bar for style options

Body of note

Note @ Bury

Note Content

To the left, you can see the main note creation page. This lets you attach audio and images. When you scroll the options bar, you can also add style options such as bold and italics.

Tag

Select notebooks

Take photo

Done

Audio

Attach item

See all of your notes

Create a new note

Search

Menu

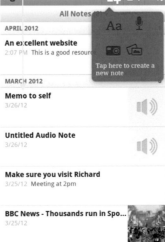

To the right, you can see all of the notes you have taken. It is possible to create a new note from this page or search the existing ones.

...cont'd

Don't forget

It is not possible to create new checkboxes in notes when using Evernote on the BlackBerry so you cannot produce checklists or task lists.

122

BlackBerry

The BlackBerry version of Evernote has a similar frontend interface to Android. Using large icons, you can speedily navigate to the required sections of the app.

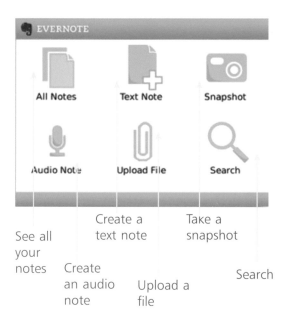

See all your notes

Create a text note

Create an audio note

Take a snapshot

Upload a file

Search

Taking efficient snapshots on a BlackBerry phone

1   Click on the Text Note icon on your BlackBerry phone

2   Select the attachment option and you will be given three choices: snapshot, file and audio

3   Select the snapshot option and you will be able to take an image using your phone's camera

4   When you have finished taking a photo, you will be able to save it in one of four ways. You can keep it as its native size or you can select to have it small, medium or large. The smaller the note, the easier it will be to sync when on a slower connection

Windows Phone

The Windows Phone 7 version of Evernote looks different to other versions and takes on the style familiar to owners of the phone. Here we look at how you can create a note.

Be sure to tag items so that you can search for them much easier. Getting into the practice of doing this will save you lots of time in the long run.

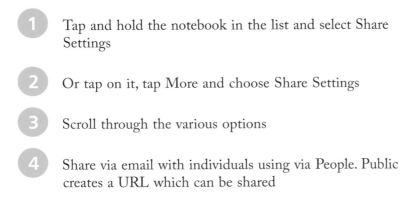

Note title   Save   Image and audio   Body text

Share a notebook with Windows Phone

1 Tap and hold the notebook in the list and select Share Settings

2 Or tap on it, tap More and choose Share Settings

3 Scroll through the various options

4 Share via email with individuals using via People. Public creates a URL which can be shared

...cont'd

Hot tip

To share a note that you are working on, you must save it first. Then you can share it in the usual way.

Apple iPad

Using the large screen of the iPad, Evernote shows a series of large blocks, drawn to look like pages from a notebook.

Edit: tap here to delete or share a note

See all notes

See tags or view shared items and notebooks

Tap More to see Places and Searches

Create a note

Sort by date, title, notebook, city or country

Settings

10 Using SocialFolders

As well as being able to store items in the cloud, you can also download them. SocialFolders lets you back up your social media.

Back up your social media

If you invite a friend to join SocialFolders, you will be allowed to connect to another service and work with another 1,000 file transfers per month.

Social media such as Facebook, Twitter, Flickr and YouTube have had a major impact on our lives. We can see what our friends and family are up to, watch videos and view images posted by others and send public messages around the world.

In doing so, we are sending out lots of information and being bombarded with lots of media. Using a service such as SocialFolders, we can keep copies of this kind of data and store it on our hard drives.

In many ways, it is reverse cloud computing: taking what is out there and bringing it closer to home. But it is a way of keeping a back-up on your own hard drive and having all your social media data in one place. You could, if you wish, then copy it all to a service such as Dropbox, thereby taking from the cloud and putting it back elsewhere.

SocialFolders works with a host of social media including:

- Twitter
- Facebook
- Google Docs
- Evernote
- Instagram
- YouTube
- Picasa
- SmugMug
- Photobucket

To use SocialFolders, you need to have an app installed on your Windows PC or Mac.

It places an icon in the system tray of your PC and in the menu bar of a Mac computer.

You can then choose which social media you wish to link with. Then, when you upload an image, for example, it will sync automatically with your hard drive.

Create a SocialFolders account

1 Go to the SocialFolders website at socialfolders.me

2 Click Download on the homepage

3 SocialFolders will detect if you are running a PC or Mac and it will start to download the app

4 Run the app to install it

5 Tell the app where you would like to have it install

6 You will be asked to sign up for the service so fill in your name and choose a password

Sign-Up

Sign up for SocialFolders

First name David
Last name Crookes
Email david
Password
Confirm password

☐ I have read and agree to the Terms of Service.

Already have an account?

Go Back   Continue

7 The app will set up an account and you will receive an email verification

8 An icon will appear in your PC's system tray or on your Mac's menu bar

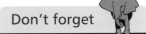

Don't forget

When SocialFolders has installed, a folder called SocialFolders is created in your local Documents folder on a PC. On a Mac, a shortcut is added to the Finder sidebar.

127

Connect to your services

Before you can start to use SocialFolders, you need to tell it to hook up to your social media accounts:

1 Right-click on the icon in your PC's system tray or Mac's menu bar

2 Select Connect to my services

3 SocialFolders will open in your web browser. It will detect that you have never connected one of your services. Click on Connect to your first service

> Looks like you've never connected to one of your services.
>
> Connect to your first service ▶

4 You will see a large number of services from Evernote to Facebook to Google Docs. Choose the one you wish to connect with. In this instance, we will use Facebook

5 A window will open asking you for your log in details for that particular service. Type them in

6 Depending on the service, you may be asked to grant SocialFolders permission to access your account. If you are agreeable, then go ahead

7 SocialFolders will begin to gather data. It may ask you if you want to import items. For example, with Facebook, it will ask if you want to download your photos

8 You can now go back and connect to other services

Limitations

The free version only allows you to connect up to three services at a time. If you want more, then you will have to pay, although you do get awarded with an additional service connect if you recommend a friend. You are also limited to 2,000 photos, documents and other files.

Beware

If the SocialFolders icon is black it means there is a network problem.

Hot tip

If a file is added to a social network twice via different means at roughly the same time, e.g. via a computer and a website, then it will be marked as conflict. Just rename or remove to solve the issue.

Viewing your files

Beware

You cannot delete files or folders through SocialFolders. You need to delete them from the site they came from.

Hot tip

Copy a file from one social network to another by dragging it from folder to folder within SocialFolders.

Now that you have started to connect your social media services, you will want to see what is happening to them on your hard drive:

1 Go to the icon in your PC's system tray or Mac's menu bar and right-click it

2 Select Open SocialFolders

3 You will see that SocialFolders has created a folder. What type of folder it is will depend on the service you connected to

4 Open the folder and you will see sub-folders

5 These folders will contain data from the services that you have connected to. For example, you would be able to see your Facebook profile pictures, mobile uploads, any photos you are tagged in and any other albums you have set up

6 Clicking on an item in the folder will enable you to open it. The item resides on your hard drive and it will work like any other file of its type

Download your friend's data

You are not only limited to syncing your own folders. You can also download those of your friend's on services such as Facebook, Flickr and Twitter:

1. Log in to your account at socialfolders.me

2. Click on the Flickr, Twitter or Facebook option

3. We are going to use Facebook as an example. As well as the My Albums option, you can also choose Friends. Click on this and you will see all of the people that you are friends with on Facebook

131

4. By the side of each of your friends, you will see a downward pointing arrow. When you click on this, it will show the albums your friend has posted on Facebook

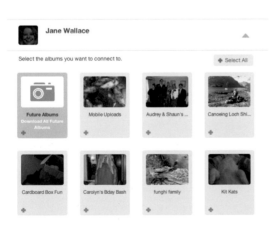

5. You can choose Select All or click the cross on each album. It will turn green

6. Click on the SocialFolders icon on your PC or Mac and select Refresh all my services. Your friend's folders will appear

Upload photos in one go

Although the primary aim of SocialFolders is to allow you to sync and store files from social media on your computer, you can also take large numbers of files and upload them:

1 Find an image folder on your hard drive that you wish to copy

2 Open SocialFolders by clicking on the icon in your system tray (PC) or menu bar (Mac)

3 Select Open SocialFolders

4 Find the folder of the service you wish to upload to and navigate to the folder in which your other picture albums are kept

5 Drag and drop your image folder into SocialFolders

6 When SocialFolders is refreshed, your images are uploaded. Your pictures will be online a few minutes later

11 Task management

It's not always easy to remember things so imagine if you could store your thoughts on a remote server amd have them to hand whenever you need a reminder. With Remember The Milk you can effectively manage all of your day-to-day tasks with ease.

Your memory in the cloud

We cannot remember everything. That's why we have pens and paper. Jotting things down gives us a little reminder that we have to do something. The only problem is that you are then reliant on having that scrap of paper with you. And paper, can easily get lost, wet or crumpled. It's not the most robust of systems.

In this section, we are going to look at an application called Remember The Milk. There are other similar apps but this is an easy one to use and it is also powerful. The fact it can sync your tasks across the internet allows you to pick up your lists on computers and mobile devices wherever you have an internet connection. Its reminder service will also prompt you so that you will not forget that crucial task. Like the bottle of milk you were supposed to pick up from the supermarket on your way home.

The benefits of Remember The Milk are plentiful:

- You can get your reminders by email, SMS or instant messaging so that remembering becomes easy

- You can manage your tasks offline

- There are mobile apps which make sure keeping up with task management is never a logistical nightmare

- You can use it in combination with Google Calendar

- And it is free

Join Remember The Milk

1   Go to rememberthemilk.com and click Sign Up Now! on the homepage

2   Fill in your name, username, password and email address

3   Choose the date format which looks right for you. Tick the terms and conditions box and click Sign Up

4   You will be sent a verification code by email so click on the link to complete the sign-up process

Hot tip

It is good practice to only allow your computer to remember your login details if you are sure your machine is secure. In any case, the Remember The Milk cookie lasts for just two weeks before it prompts you to re-login. Click Logout at the top of the screen to sign off.

remember the milk

Home   Sign Up (Free!)   Services   Blog   Help

Sign Up

Sign up with your Google Account

First Name		⊗ First name is required
Last Name		
Username		
Password		
Confirm Password		
Email Address		
Which Looks Right	○ 14/02/11 ○ 02/14/11	
	☐ I have read and accept the Terms of Use.	
	Sign Up	

Verification email

1   When your verification email arrives you will be asked to click a link to complete the sign-up process

2   But make a note too of the email address it gives you. It takes the format of: username+code@milk.com. This address will allow you to create task and reminder information for Remember The Milk by sending an email

Create a task online

We look at the steps of creating a task with Remember The Milk using the service's website:

1 Log in at rememberthemilk.com

2 Type an instruction into the main task bar

3 When you hit Enter, you will see a box on the right-hand side giving you more options for better management

4 Click on the calendar and you can enter a date. You could put Jan 2, for instance, or write tomorrow or next Wednesday. Remember The Milk understands

5 There are other options too:

This icon lets you choose to repeat a reminder

You can decide on a time scale, say 30 minutes

Edit a note

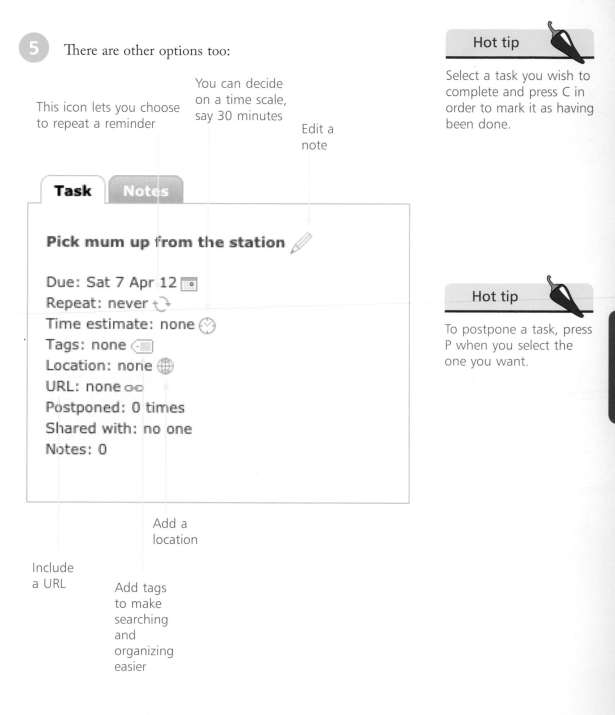

Task   Notes

Pick mum up from the station 🖉

Due: Sat 7 Apr 12 ▦
Repeat: never ↻
Time estimate: none ⊘
Tags: none ⬛
Location: none ⊕
URL: none ∞
Postponed: 0 times
Shared with: no one
Notes: 0

137

Add a location

Include a URL

Add tags to make searching and organizing easier

Manage locations

It is possible to add and manage locations with Remember The Milk. These are then displayed on a Google map for reference.

Use a street address

1 Click on the Locations option from the menu bar that runs across the top of the website

2 You will see an entry box. Type in the street address or a place name and click Go

3 The address will be shown on the map

4 A box will appear on the map. Type in the location here and press Enter

Use the map

1 Find an area on the map and click Add Location

2 Click on the map area that you want to add

3 Type in the location in the box that appears and press the Enter key on your keyboard

Set up reminders

Reminders can be received in a variety of ways, making Remember The Milk a versatile system.

You can choose to have them sent by:

- Email
- AIM
- GaduGadu
- GoogleTalk
- ICQ
- Jabber
- MSN
- Skype
- Yahoo
- Mobile

Settings menu

1   Click on Settings and choose the Reminders tab. You will now see the options available to you

Beware

Not every network provider will allow you to receive text reminders so check if yours will by going to rememberthemilk.com/help/answers/reminders/smsnetworks.rtm.

Beware

Some networks charge for SMS reminders but most do not. Remember The Milk does not charge anything for the service.

...cont'd

Hot tip

If a reminder is not being received by email, then check your junk folder just in case.

2 You can set up a daily reminder by ticking the box next to the words On the day the task is due

3 If you tick the next box, you can specify a timescale. For example, you could write 30 minutes

Send me a daily reminder...
- ☑ On the day the task is due
- ☑ [30 minutes] before the task is due

Send daily reminders at [9am]

4 Tasks which have a due time can also be set. You can ask to be reminded at the time a task is due or a set time before it is due

If the task has a due time, remind me...
- ☑ At the time the task is due
- ☐ [   ] before the task is due

[Save Changes] [Cancel]

5 Save Changes to finish

How do you want to be reminded?

1 Use the drop-down box to toggle through the options

2 Select a service and fill in the email or username associated with that account. For example, use your Skype ID if you want to be reminded by Skype

3 When choosing Mobile, select your carrier. Fill in your phone number and select a daily message limit if you want one

Share your tasks

Let other people view your task by sharing it with them. This will also allow them to change it if they wish:

1 Select the task you want to share

2 Click on More Actions and in the drop-down menu select Share With

3 Your contacts will be displayed. If you have no contacts yet, click on the Add Contact option. You can invite a contact to join Remember The Milk if they are not a member already

4 Click Share and you will see, in your tasks list, that the task you selected is now being shared

What if someone shares with you?

1 A notification will appear in your Overview section

2 To accept or reject it, click on Settings and go to Lists

3 Select the items you want and in the box on the right either accept or reject the offer

Beware

Once a task is shared, you cannot unshare it.

Hot tip

Tasks shared with you will appear in your inbox.

Create a Smart List

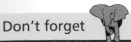
You can create lists of tasks according to search results. These can then form what are called Smart Lists. You can produce Smart Lists for a whole range of criteria. Maybe you want to create a list according to a keyword contained in your tags or have a list according to a due date for a task:

1 Perform a search. For better results, ensure you click on Show Search Options

2 On the right-hand side of the screen you will see the search results under the List tab

List	Save

🖶 **Print**

**Search Results
(3 tasks)**

Searched for: tag:travel

0 due today
2 due tomorrow
0 overdue
30 minutes estimated
0 completed

3 Click on the Save tab

4 Give the list a name – for example Travel – and Save

5 The new Smart List will be added to the tabs which run along the top of the main window. The new tab will be coloured blue

Inbox **Personal** Study Work Sent **All Tasks** **Travel**

Using email to submit tasks

As well as being self-contained, Remember The Milk will also let you email tasks to it.

When you signed up, your verification email highlighted your unique Remember The Milk email address.

But if you go to Settings and click Info you can also see it there. The email takes the form of your username+code@milk.com.

Beware

You cannot change your unique Remember The Milk email address.

Using the email subject line

1 Open your email client

2 Enter your Remember The Milk email in the To field

3 You can use the subject line to send yourself a task. For example, you could write:

Hot tip

Remember The Milk advises anyone who has an email client that does not support a "+" character to replace this in their email address with "%2b".

- Buy a present for Jane

  This will send a message to your Remember The Milk account, adding it to your list of tasks

- Buy a present for Jane on June 15 at 9am

  This will send a message and include time and date information

4 You can also add notes. Place these in the email body and separate each note by three hyphens (---)

5 There are some symbols you can use for even better control over your task:

- Use * to denote frequency, so *daily

- Use = to denote a timescale, so =30min

- Use # to denote the type of list or a tag, so #travel

Hot tip

Private addresses have to be turned on before you can proceed. Go to Settings, click the General tab and next to Private Addresses press On. Now Save.

Sync with Google Calendar

Remember The Milk lets you create a feed which can be used with Google Calendar. Any tasks you create with Remember The Milk will appear within your Google Calendar on the required date.

In Remember The Milk

1 Log in to your Remember The Milk account

2 Click Settings

3 Select the General tab

4 Next to Private Addresses, make sure you click the circle next to On and then Save Changes

5 Now go to your list on the right-hand side of the screen. You will see an option for iCalendar (Events)

6 Right-click iCalendar (Events) and select Copy Shortcut (or Copy Link Location on a Mac)

In Google Calendar

1 Log in to Google Calendar

2 In the left-hand column next to Other Calendars, click the drop-down arrow and select Add by URL

3 Right-click in the window which appears and select Paste. The URL will be copied

4 To finish, click Add Calendar in the window. A new calendar will appear containing your Remember The Milk event information

Using Twitter with Remember The Milk

You can use your Twitter account to send tasks direct to Remember The Milk.

Don't forget

Need a list of commands for Twitter? Go to http://www.rememberthemilk.com/services/twitter/ and see a comprehensive list.

In Remember The Milk

1 Go to rememberthemilk.com/services/twitter

2 On the right-hand side, input your Twitter username

3 Press submit and you will receive a code. Highlight this, right-click it and copy

4 Highlight the code, right-click it and copy. Alternatively, write it down. You will need this for the next steps

In Twitter

1 Log into your Twitter account

2 Find and follow @rtm

3 Create a new tweet. Write d rtm and the code. For example, d rtm 3m67. This will send a direct message to Remember The Milk

4 Now if you want to send a task to Remember The Milk, create a tweet. Always start it with d rtm unless you are already on the direct message web page. Press Tweet to send it

5 You can type in a message just as you would from the Remember The Milk website. For example: pick up mum from station today

Don't forget

The address is m.rememberthemilk.com – there are no wwws.

Using a smartphone

There are various ways of gaining access to the information stored in the cloud via Remember The Milk on your phone or tablet.

Apps are available for:

- Android via Google Play
- iPhone via App Store
- iPad via App Store

These are free to download and use.

Mobile internet version of Remember The Milk

As well as dedicated apps, you can view Remember The Milk via a browser on a smartphone. The screen is optimized for the smaller size of a phone:

1   Go to m.rememberthemilk.com

2   Log in with your username and password

3   You will see a menu. You can choose to view your tasks for today, tomorrow and this week. You can also see lists, tags and perform a search

4   Add a task by choosing option 9. Input the task name, choose a list, mark a priority, choose a date and time estimate, enter tags, a location and URL before tapping Add Task

12 Pictures in the cloud

Keep your cherished moments safe and sound and share them with others.

Set up and use Flickr

Flickr is a popular photo website which allows you to upload your images and share them through Facebook, Twitter, email and many more. You can also see photos taken by other people.

Flickr is great because:

- You can upload photos via the web, your phone or tablet, email or an image package

- You can view and share them wherever you are

- You can become inspired by the images of others

And finally:

- It is free

Signing up

1. Go to flickr.com

2. Click Create New Account or sign in with your Facebook, Google or Yahoo! ID

3. If creating a new account, you'll need to set up a Yahoo email address and add some security questions

4. Flickr will ask you to specify a screen name

5. You are now ready to personalize your profile and upload

Hot tip

Flickr makes use of Creative Commons licenses. This lets you set the level of freedom you wish someone to have with your images.

There are four types: Attribution (where a credit is asked for), NonCommercial (allowing only for non-commercial use), NoDerivs (no one is allowed to alter the work) and ShareAlike (it has to be shared in the same way). If you choose All Rights Reserved no-one else can distribute your photos or videos.

Uploading photos

The Flickr user interface is simple to get around. The homepage shows your Photostream and contacts and there is a link to upload your images and videos:

1 Click on Upload Photos & Videos on the right-hand side of the screen when visiting the website

» Upload Photos & Video NEW

2 Click Choose photos and videos

3 Browse your hard drive for images and videos. Hold down the Control key (or Command on a Mac) to select more than one file

4 Flickr will display the files on the website. You can use the trashcan icon to remove the images

5 Now set the privacy settings. Make a choice from:

- Private so they can be viewed only by you

- Private but also visible to friends and family which gives the ability to message with friends

- Public so that anyone can view them

6 Click Upload Photos and Videos and they will be uploaded

Using Flickr tools

As well as being able to upload images to the cloud via your web browser, you can also do it via a desktop app, email and plug-ins for other apps. The tools for these can be found at http://www.flickr.com/tools/.

Desktop version

1 Go to the website above and you can choose to download the Desktop version of Flickr for Windows or Mac. Make your choice and click on the one you want

2 The app will install on your machine. Open and sign in. You will be asked to confirm that you want the Flickr Uploader to link to your account

3 To upload images and video, you can drag them to the main window or click Add to browse

4 Add a title and description and so on and then click Create A Set to upload them

Email from computer or phone

1 Go to flickr.com/account/uploadbyemail/ to see your unique email address

2 Send an image via email on your computer or select to Share an image in your phone's camera roll to this address and it will upload it

3 Use the subject line to add a title and the body to add a description for your image

Create a Flickr set

You can group images into sets for better organization and to show off your collections in a better way. This is different from a gallery which you can only make of other people's images (as long as they allow it):

1. Go to http://www.flickr.com/photos/organize/?start_tab=sets

2. Drag your content into the main box or click Create Your First Set

3. Clicking on Batch edit will let you add titles, tags and descriptions en masse. You can also do the same for filters and content type and a whole lot more. This is quicker than selecting individual files

Don't forget

Add tags to your photos so that people will be able to search for and find them.

151

4. In the top right-hand corner you will see a box which says "the photo or video you drag here will represent the set". Drag an image or film into here to produce the image that will show off your set

5. If you click on the Print & Create tab you can even produce sets of images that you can print. Flickr has a service that will allow you to have a set of images professionally printed

Create a Flickr group

It is possible to create a group that is tailored for your needs. You can produce one that is public or private or even one that is invite only. Groups come with a discussion board. You will be the administrator of your group and your invitees would be members:

State clearly your intention for the group so that people posting to it will remain relevant to the vibe you are trying to create. Why not search Flickr for relevant images that can be added to your group too?

1 Go to http://www.flickr.com/groups/

2 Click Create your own group

3 Decide what type of group you wish to set up:

- Private - great for families and friends

- Public for all

- Public for invitees only

4 Give your group a name. You can also describe what it is about and decide if it is an 18-rated group or not

5 Click Next then specify titles for members

6 Click Your Group icon to add an image that defines your group. You can also produce a unique web address by going to Flickr web address

7 To add images, click the Groups menu option at the top of the screen and select your group. There is an option to Add photos

13 Audio and video

Take your music with you wherever you go by using cloud-based music services or putting your own tracks into the cloud. You can also stream movies direct to your computer or console so you need never use a DVD or Blu-Ray ever again

Audio and video in the cloud

Don't forget

If you are streaming music to a mobile phone, you are advised to use a Wi-Fi connection for better quality and also to prevent wasting any data allowance you may have.

Remember vinyl? Cassettes? CDs? How about a MiniDisc? Or videotape? DVD? Blu-Ray? Over the years, the way we listen to our music and watch our films has changed.

Today, people listen less frequently to music stored on physical media. MP3 players are popular and digital music is king.

When it comes to movies too, we do not have to rely on the local video store and neither do we have to wait for programmes to appear on television.

For as well as downloading music or film to a device, you can also stream it. Music and film are stored on a remote computer – in the cloud – and you select songs and movies that you wish to listen to or watch. These are then delivered to a device, be it a computer, phone, MP3 player, console or streaming device.

We are going to look at four services:

- Netflix
- LoveFilm
- Spotify
- iTunes in the Cloud with iTunes Match

View films via Netflix

Netflix allows you to access hundreds of movies and television episodes each month for a set fee. It is free to try for 30 days:

 Go to netflix.com and the website will detect which country you are in

 You will see details of your free trial and an invitation to join. Input your email and password and confirm both before pressing Continue

3 On the next page fill in your name and enter your credit card or PayPal details. You will then become a member

Find a film

1 Browse the films on the Netflix website and choose one. Press play and it will begin to stream

2 Apps are available for the Nintendo Wii, Xbox 360 (you need Xbox Live Gold) and PlayStation 3 consoles. Sign in via these apps, choose a film and it will stream

3 You can download and install the Netflix app on your Android device, iPhone or iPad. Sign in and you can stream movies when you have an internet connection

Hot tip

Netflix movies can be streamed to internet-connected HD televisions made by Samsung, Apple TV, Philips streaming players and Western Digital.

Hot tip

If you do not have a streaming device, you can use a HDMI or VGA cable to connect your laptop to your television. Most modern laptops have HDMI connections as do all HD televisions. When you stream your film via your Netflix account on your laptop, it will instantly appear on your television.

Watch movies via LoveFilm

In the UK, LoveFilm is one of the top movie streaming services. Like Netflix, it allows you to subscribe for a set fee and choose from hundreds of movies:

Don't forget

Sony or Samsung internet connected TVs can directly connect to the LoveFilm service.

1 Go to lovefilm.com and select the option to sign up

2 Follow the sign-up process and input your payment details when prompted

3 The LoveFilm instant account lets you view movies on a television, PS3, Xbox 360, laptop and iPad:

- PS3: Find the LoveFilm icon on the Xross Media Bar and log in to your account.

- Xbox 360: Sign in to Xbox Live, go to My Apps and select LoveFilm. If you cannot see it, go to the Xbox Marketplace and download it to your machine

- iPad: Download the app from the App Store and sign in to your account

- PC: Go to the Watch Online section of the LoveFilm website, find a film and click Watch Now. It will immediately play. You can also connect your computer to your television (see page 155)

4 Movies are categorized according to their genre for ease of use, helping you to find a film you want

Beware

Not all films are available to view via the subscription package. Some have to be ordered for sending via mail on DVD or Blu-Ray and others attract one-off but small fees in order to watch.

Using Spotify

Spotify puts millions of songs at your disposal. You can use it on your PC, Mac or smartphone:

 Go to Spotify.com

2 Spotify has a deal with Facebook. If you are signing up for the first time, you need to connect your Facebook account with Spotify

![Spotify sign-up screen]

3 Choose the package you want (you can see a full overview at www.spotify.com/get-spotify/overview/):

- Free has adverts and does not allow phone streams

- Unlimited removes the ads and includes radio

- Premium allows you to stream songs to a phone

4 You will then be prompted to download the Spotify app for your PC or Mac

5 If you have paid for the Premium package, you will want to install the Spotify app to your phone. There are apps for iPhone and Android available from the App Store or Google Play.

6 You can also access Spotify on other mobile phones by going to m.spotify.com

Don't forget

You will need a Facebook account to sign up to Spotify. If you do not have one, you can easily create an account at facebook.com.

Beware

If you opt for the free Spotify service, you are limited to 10 hours of free streaming per month. The stream also contains adverts.

Create playlists with Spotify

Spotify makes it easy to find songs and you can also create playlists, allowing for the streaming of only the songs you like.

Hot tip

You can use some search tricks to find the songs you want by using 'year:' to specify a year. For example 'Oasis year:1995'. You could also widen this out to, say, 'Oasis year:1995-2007'.

Find a song

1 Click on the search box at the top of the Spotify app for PC or Mac and type the name of a song or artist

2 A list of songs will appear if your search is successful. Click on the one you want

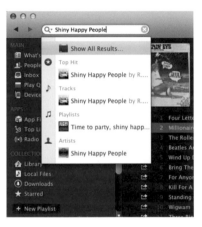

Hot tip

Want to search by genre? Then type 'genre:' and the name of the type of music you love. For a long list, go to http://spotgate.org/help/spotify_genres/all/all.shtml.

3 The song will appear in the main music area of Spotify, often within the context of an album. Double-click the song to play it

Create a playlist

1 In the left-hand menu, you will see an icon called New Playlist. Click this and a new entry is made which you can rename

2 Drag a track to the playlist to add it or right-click a track and select Add To

Share Spotify playlists

The cloud nature of Spotify makes it easy to share a song with other people:

 Open a playlist and click the Share icon

 A window will appear. You can share it on Facebook, Twitter or Messenger or allow another Spotify user to enjoy it

 Select which service you want and send it. Sample text will appear which you can alter

 If you want to share a particular song, you can right click on it and scroll down to select Share to

		Track	Get	Artist	Time
★	↪	Everybody Hurts	⬇	R.E.M.	5:18
	↪	Nightswimming	⬇	R.E.M.	4:16
	↪	Imitation Of Life	⬇	R.E.M.	3:57
	↪	Losing My Religion	⬇	R.E.M.	4:27
★	↪	Man On The M		R.E.M.	5:14
	↪	Bad Day		R.E.M.	4:06
	↪	What's The Fre		R.E.M.	4:00
	↪	Shiny Happy Pe		R.E.M.	3:43
	↪	Daysleeper		R.E.M.	3:39
	↪	The Sidewinde		R.E.M.	4:08

Play
Go to Replacement

Queue
Start Radio
Add To   ▶
Star

5 Plays Left
Get Track

Copy HTTP Link
Copy Spotify URI
Share to...

Delete

Hot tip

You can share songs via email and even link to an exact position within the song. Copy the Spotify URL and replace the hash tag with %23. At the end of the URL type "#time" where time is the location of part of the track such as 1:15.

159

Don't forget

These song services are 100 per cent legal but there are some less legitimate websites on the internet, some of which could infect your computer with a virus.

Spotify on a smartphone

Although all users can download and use the Spotify app for iPhone and Android or access m.spotify.com via other smartphones, you need to be a Premium member to stream songs:

1   Use the search bar at the top of the screen to look for new songs

2   If you are not a Premium user, the songs will be grayed out. To listen you will have to upgrade your account

3   The Playlists icon on your phone will show you all of the songs you already have available to stream

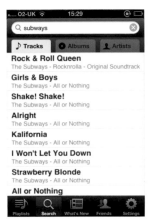

4   Pick one of your playlists and it will stream songs to your smartphone

5   By going to the Settings menu within the Spotify app, you can turn the Offline Mode On. This will allow any playlists that you have made available for offline listening to be played, saving on data costs and ensuring a smooth playback

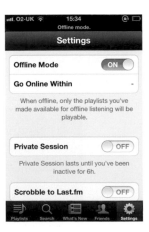

6   If you want to be kept abreast of the top tracks and new releases, then you should tap What's New on your app. You can access this no matter what level of subscription you are on and you can also read Spotify's news feed

Using iTunes in the cloud

Using iCloud, it is possible to have your music made available on any of the devices on which you run iTunes. New music purchases as well as past ones are stored. These are then automatically downloaded without the hassle of syncing:

1. On your iOS device, tap on your Settings icon

2. Scroll down to Store

3. Turn Automatic Downloads for Music on

4. On your computer, whether a PC or Mac, open iTunes

5. Click Edit>Preferences on a PC or iTunes>Preferences on a Mac and click on the Store tab

6. Decide if you want to always check for available downloads by checking the box

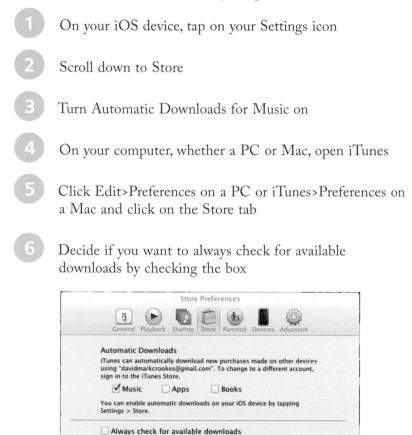

7. If the options are grayed out, it means you have not signed in to the iTunes store. It may also be that your computer is not authorized for use with your Apple ID, in which case go to Store>Authorize This Computer

Hot tip

If you have an iPhone or iPod touch with tiny storage space, iTunes in the Cloud will give it a major boost.

Download songs to a device

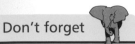

Don't forget

Once you have bought a song on iTunes, it is yours to keep. If you delete it, you are able to re-download it at no extra cost.

If a song that is contained in your iTunes account is not on one of your iOS devices, you can quickly download it. This pulls the song from the cloud:

1. Open up iTunes on your iOS device, whether an iPhone, iPod touch or iPad

2. Where you see a cloud icon next to a song, you can tap it to download

3. You will be asked for your password and the song will then download to your device

4. You can now play the song

Using iTunes Match

One downside to using iTunes in the Cloud is its inability to store all of your music. Only songs which you have bought from iTunes are stored. Except, that is, if you pay for a service called iTunes Match. This allows you to store your whole collection. So if you have music on CDs or if you bought from another service such as Amazon, you can have all the benefits of iTunes in the Cloud for all of your music.

What's the Match part?

iTunes Match does more than just store your tunes. It takes the non-iTunes purchased songs and looks on its system for the direct equivalent. If it finds it, it will swap it for its own high-quality version running at 256Kbps in AAC format and with no DRM attached. It will even swap lower quality copies for better sounding ones. The only songs it will not match are those that are not in the iTunes system. These will be uploaded from your own source instead:

Beware

You can only link up to 10 devices to one iTunes Match account.

163

 Go to apple.com/itunes/itunes-match/ or click on iTunes Match in the left-hand menu of iTunes

2 The iTunes Match service will open in the iTunes Store

3 Click on the Subscribe button to purchase an iTunes Match subscription

Uploading to iTunes Match

Once you have subscribed to iTunes Match, you are ready to start uploading songs. This, however, is an automatic process.

How it works

1 When you set your subscription for the first time, iTunes Match will:

- Gather information about your iTunes library

- Match your music with songs in the iTunes Store

- Upload artwork and remaining songs

iTunes Match

Step 1: Gathering information about your iTunes library.
Step 2: Matching your music with songs in the iTunes Store.
Step 3: Uploading artwork and remaining songs.

You can continue using iTunes while iTunes Match is in progress.

iTunes Match

Step 1: Gathering information about your iTunes library.
Step 2: Matching your music with songs in the iTunes Store.
Step 3: Uploading artwork and remaining songs.

11 of 605 Songs Checked

You can continue using iTunes while iTunes Match is in progress.

2 Go to Settings on your iOS 5 device, tap Music and turn on iTunes Match

Settings	**Music**	
iTunes Match		ON
Shake to Shuffle		ON
Sound Check		OFF
EQ		Off >
Volume Limit		Off >
Lyrics & Podcast Info		ON
Group By Album Artist		ON

Home Sharing

Apple ID   example@me.com

3 You will now be able to access your songs on an iPhone, iPod touch or iPad

14 Playing in the cloud

The cloud does not have to be work, work, work. With OnLive and Gaikai you are able to stream some of the best blockbuster games to most web-enabled computers and play them without having to own any high-end equipment or bother with consoles and physical media.

Understanding cloud gaming

Cloud gaming is an exciting development which allows games to be delivered over the internet. The games themselves are stored "in the cloud" on remote servers and the player chooses a title via a front-end user interface which is displayed locally, on a computer, phone or tablet.

When a player uses a controller to interact with a game, information about which keys have been pressed or the direction a stick has been pushed is sent to the remote server. The required action is performed in the game and the player sees the end result on their own screen.

The key to the technology is that the player is seeing a video of the game being played on that remote server. That is, the game's graphics are being converted to video which is then streamed to a player's own device via the internet.

One of the benefits of this is the ability to play cutting edge games on even the most basic of machines. All that is required is an account to a service such as OnLive and an internet connection. This will then give the player access to dozens and dozens of top games.

This is great because:

- You do not need a cutting edge system to play the best and latest games

- You have access to a vast library of titles without having to go to the shops or order a disk online

- You can buy a subscription which covers you for multiple games which will save you money

- You can stop playing a game on one system and resume it on another. No download is required

But...

- It is important to have a reasonably fast connection otherwise the video compression may appear blocky

- There can be some lag – that is, you notice a time delay in pressing a button and the action being performed

Playing with OnLive

OnLive claims to be the pioneer of on-demand, instant-play videogame services. It has a large number of top-rated blockbuster games for you to try.

It allows you to play games on:

- A PC
- A Mac
- A television with the OnLive games system
- A tablet or smartphone

You can start a game on one of these devices and continue playing on another.

Players can sign up to OnLive for free and play demos and some games but there are paid-for options:

- The PlayPack has dozens of games available and it costs a small amount each month
- You can also buy individual titles at a variety of costs

The PlayPack tends to include older games but if you are happy with that, then it is a cost-effective way of gaining access to a wealth of titles, some of them classic retro ones.

Don't forget

You can hook up a controller to your computer or device and play your games just as you would if using a Xbox, PlayStation or Nintendo console.

You can use an Xbox 360 controller as well as a Logitech ChillStream, Logitech F510, Saitek P3200 Rumble Pad and a Mad Catz GamePad.

167

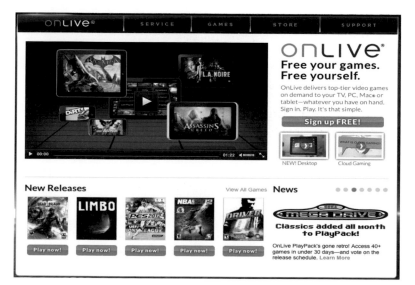

Beware

For security, do not input a username that relates to your real name or could otherwise identify you.

Signing up to OnLive

You can sign up to OnLive via the service's website. You do not have to pay any money at this stage. It is a good opportunity to become familiar with the set-up of OnLive:

1 Go to the OnLive website at onlive.com or onlive.co.uk on your PC or Mac

2 Click on the 'Sign Up FREE' option in the top right of the screen

3 Enter your email address

4 Create a new password

5 Create a Player Tag. This is like a username and it will be used to identify you.

6 Input your date of birth

7 Decide whether or not you want to be emailed by OnLive and agree to the terms of service, the privacy policy and community guidelines

8 Click Finish

9 You will be taken straight to your account. Click on the first option Complete your Profile

10 Click on Update Profile. You can now include your Play Style (Casual, Family, Enthusiast, Hardcore) and a motto

11 Click Save when done

Setting up OnLive billing

You may be interested in some of the paid-for services such as the monthly subscription or a one-off game. You will need to set up your billing account in order to pay:

1. Log in to OnLive and select Account at the top of the screen

2. Click on Billing in the account menu bar

3. On the left-hand side of the screen, click on the words Enter a Credit Card

4. Fill in your billing address

5. Add your credit card details

6. When you have finished, click Save

Don't forget

You can play 30 minutes of any game for free without the need for a credit card.

169

Update Billing Information

BILLING ADDRESS

Address:

| Address Line1 |
| Address Line2 |
| City |

United Kingdom | State/Province/Region | Zip/Postal

Phone Number:

CREDIT CARD

Cardholder Name:

| Name |

Card Type:

Select Card | VISA

Card Number: | CVV:

Credit Card Number |

Expiration Date:

Month | Year

Cancel | Save

The card you are entering will be the default card on file for your Account. You can change your default card at onlive.co.uk/account/billing. You will only be charged for services and products purchased under your Account.

Purchasing on onlive.co.uk is only available to customers in the United Kingdom. Customers in the United States and Canada should visit onlive.com. We continue to work towards making the service available in other countries.

Set OnLive parental controls

If you are a parent or a guardian and you wish to control what your children are playing, you will need to delve into the parental control options within OnLive:

1 Click Account and go to Parental Controls

2 Select Set Parental Controls

3 You need to set up a password. It must be between six and 16 characters and it has to be different from your main log in

4 You will see two columns: Content Control and Online Privacy and Safety Settings

Content Control

1 Click edit at the bottom of the Content Control column

2 Choose the rating you wish to limit the games to and then decide if you want to allow unrated or Rating Pending games

3 You can enter the specific titles of games you wish to allow through the filter. Click Save

Content Control Settings

Allow Games By Rating
Allow games with these ratings:

3, 7, 12 rated games

3 7 12 16 18

☐ Allow unrated or Rating Pending Games

Allow Specific Games
Enter specific game titles below, or select and remove games from the allow list.

Cancel   Save

Privacy and Safety Settings

1 Click Edit at the bottom of the Online Privacy and Safety Settings column

2 You can select if you want to allow Social Features and Privacy. These are:

- The ability to manage your friends list
- The ability to message with friends
- The ability to voice chat with anyone
- The ability to share content with friends
- The ability to play online multiplayer games
- The ability to send alerts to friends
- The ability to have your profile viewed by friends

3 You can also select to allow or block Member Created Content. These are:

- The ability to watch or create Brag Clip videos
- Spectate live gameplay

Hot tip

Invite friends to join OnLive and you will be able to play against or with them over an internet connection.

171

Installing on PC or Mac

The beauty of cloud gaming is that you can play on any PC or Mac, no matter how lacking in power it may be. In order to start playing, however, you need to install a small app via your web browser:

 Log in to your account via a browser. Click Play in the top right-hand corner of your browser

2 On the left-hand side of the screen, it will say Get ready to play instantly. Underneath this will be a button which says Install App. Click it

3 You will be prompted to install the app so agree

4 OnLive will then take you through the installation process. This entails agreeing to the license, selecting a destination and choosing the installation type (you will want to choose a standard install)

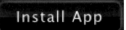

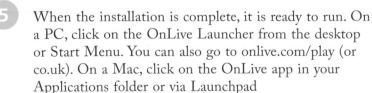

5 When the installation is complete, it is ready to run. On a PC, click on the OnLive Launcher from the desktop or Start Menu. You can also go to onlive.com/play (or co.uk). On a Mac, click on the OnLive app in your Applications folder or via Launchpad

Playing on PC or Mac

Once you have installed your app, you are ready to play:

1 Launch the app (see step 5 on the opposite page)

2 Sign in using your email address and password

3 You will be connected to OnLive

4 If you are connected via Wi-Fi, it will recommend that you switch to a wired connection. This will give you a more fluid experience

Control method

You will see the OnLive dashboard. Getting around it is easy. It is also simple to play games. You can:

- Use the mouse to click on the options of the OnLive dashboard

- Use keyboard shortcuts to go direct to an option, for example pressing Esc to go back or Enter to select. The keyboard shortcuts are displayed clearly on the screen

- Play games using a controller

- Combine a keyboard and mouse (some games require you to do this)

Dealing with virus warnings

Some anti-virus packages will inform you that there is a threat to your machine when you are downloading OnLive.

Simply accept OnLive as a known program and continue and the problem will be resolved.

You will not have an issue with viruses by streaming games via the OnLive service.

Hot tip

Although you can play perfectly well via Wi-Fi, signals fluctuate. This is why OnLive recommends you use a wired connection when playing on a PC or Mac.

Hot tip

You will notice some games require the use of a keyboard and mouse since the titles on OnLive are the PC versions. You can hook these up to your MicroConsole via a TV adapter which is available from OnLive.

Play OnLive via your TV

If you like big-screen gaming and the comfort of sitting on a comfortable sofa in your living room while you play, then you will be pleased to know you can also play OnLive cloud gaming services via your television.

You will need:

- A high definition television which has a HDMI port. You could use the OnLive Component Video Adapter which is optional

- A wired broadband connection that has a speed of at least 3Mbps. Alternatively you will need a Powerline coax or Wi-Fi bridge

You will then need to obtain the OnLive Game System which gives you:

- The OnLive MicroConsole. This is a small box which plugs into your TV

- A wireless controller and a rechargable battery

- A power adapter, HDMI cable, ethernet cable, USB cable and two AA batteries

What you need to do

1. Connect the MicroConsole to your television using the HDMI cable

2. Connect the MicroConsole to your home internet network using the ethernet cable

3. Insert the controller battery and plug the power adapter into your MicroConsole

4. Tune your TV into the MicroConsole by looking for the relevant HDMI slot. You should see the OnLive sign-in screen

5 Sign in to OnLive using your email address and password

6 You will now see the OnLive dashboard

7 Sync the controller by following the instructions you will see on the screen and press the A button to continue

8 Calibrate the screen for the best appearance by again following the instructions on the screen and pressing A to continue when prompted

Turning the MicroConsole off

1 Press the OnLive button on your controller

2 This brings up the service page. Select Power Down

3 Confirm the selection and the MicroConsole will turn off

Play OnLive on the move

It is possible to play or view OnLive games on an iPad or smartphone using the available apps.

Android

You need at least Android 2.3 (Gingerbread) in order to use the OnLive Android app:

1. Go to Google Play on your Android device and search for OnLive

2. Click install

3. Launch the app and sign in

4. If you have an Android tablet running at least 3.1 Honeycomb, you may be able to use the OnLive Wireless Controller to play games. See the description on the app page in Google Play for the current list of tested devices

Apple

You can watch other people playing games on your Apple iPad although you are not yet able to play games yourself on the device:

1. Go to the App Store on your iPad and search for OnLive Viewer

2. Click Free, then install, signing in to your App Store account

3. Launch the app and sign in

4. You can now view games being played by other people via OnLive

The OnLive Dashboard

Whether you are viewing OnLive on a PC, Mac, TV or tablet, the dashboard is essentially the same. It contains:

- Arena. This shows you footage of people who are currently playing online

- Profile. This lets you see all of your games, friends and brag clips. You can also read your messages

- Marketplace. You can look for new games, play 30 minutes for free or make a purchase

- Showcase. All the latest OnLive news is here

- My Games. All of your games and personal achievements are in this section

- Last Played. Shows the games you last played

- Brag Clips. These are 10 second recordings of moments that you or others want to show off

- Friends. You can see what your friends are doing and see their profiles and send them a message

- Settings. You can toggle OnLive's settings

Hot tip

To see the actions available on your controller or the keyboard/mouse combination, open the Dashboard when you are playing a game.

Select a game

Don't forget

Games stored in the My Games section of the OnLive Dashboard are placed in order of when you last played them.

Now we are going to look at the fun part – actually getting a game up and running on your screen:

1 Select Marketplace from the dashboard main menu

2 You will see that many of the games have a free trial available and that there are options to make a purchase

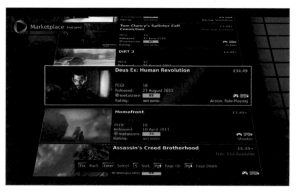

3 Highlight and click on the game that you wish to play

4 The next page contains lots of information. It details the controls, the release date and the genre as well as lots of trailers, brag clips, extras, add-ons, achievements and an average rating

5 In the top right-hand corner you will see buttons for Get Game and Free Trial. Click Free Trial, or if you are happy to buy, Get Game

6 When you click Free Trial, the game starts instantly

7 Clicking Get Game will show the purchase options. For example, there are three-day, five-day and full PlayPasses available at varying rates. Enter your password and, if you have entered your billing details, the game will be ready to play

Produce a Brag Clip

If you pull off a great move in a game, you may want to show it off to all of your friends and anyone else who views your profile. It is the equivalent of standing by an arcade machine while people stand around in awe of your skill:

Don't forget

You can have up to 50 Brag Clips in your account at any one time. Older ones are deleted when the limit is exceeded.

1 When you see an inspiring in-game move you have made that you want to keep and brag about, you can do one of three things to record the last 10 seconds of play:

- OnLive Wireless Controller: Press the Record button

- Computer: Press Alt+B on the keyboard

- Normal gamepad. Press the Center+B buttons

2 The last 10 seconds of your gameplay will then be captured

![Brag Clip Videos screen showing a grid of game clips including Borderlands, Lego Batman, Split/Second, Saints Row 2, and Ceville]

Playback

To see your Brag Clips, you need to log in to the OnLive service and then go to the Brag Clips page via the Dashboard. Select the clip you wish to view and it will play. You can view other people's clips from here too.

Find friends on OnLive

Part of the fun of OnLive is sharing your achievements and hooking up with friends:

1 Click on the Friends option from the dashboard

2 If you know the player tag or email address of a friend, click Add a Friend

3 You will be asked to enter a Player Tag or email as well as an optional message. An invite is then sent. The Friend will be added when the invite has been accepted

Add a Friend

Please enter a valid Player Tag or email address.

> dd

You may also send a message with your Friend invite.

> Type your message here

By adding a friend, you will be sharing the games you play and your profile information with that friend according to your account's current privacy settings. You can change your privacy settings in the Dashboard > Settings > Privacy.

Cancel	Add

Messages

You can send and read messages sent to and from friends:

1 Send: Select a friend in the Friends area and press Send Message. Write it and Send

2 View: Go to your profile, select the Messages option and select a friend from the list to view any messages from them. Reply, delete or let it remain on the system

3 Launch the app and sign in

4 You can now view games being played by other people via OnLive

Set up audio chat

1. To chat while gaming, launch the app and click on the main OnLive button on the dashboard (the one in the middle)

2. Scroll through the windows until you reach Settings and select Voice Chat

3. Click Voice Chat Setup

4. Click Select Output Device and choose the one you wish to use

5. It will ask you to record your voice and then play it back. Hit Record when you are ready

6. Once it has made a recording, you can hit Play. If it is not loud enough, adjust the volume and then try again

7. Click Next and the set up is complete. You can now use the Voice Chat settings to turn voice chat and the speaking indicator on or off and allow chat during single or multiplayer games

⚙ Voice Chat Beta

☒ Enable listen only
☒ Enable speaking indicator

Allow spectators to chat with me during:

☒ Single player games
☐ Multiplayer games

Volume ────────●────

Voice Chat Setup

Done

Configure Input

1. Please select the input device you would like to use.

VoIPVoice USB Phone

2. Record your voice and then play it back.

Playback   [Record]   [Play]

Level   ────────────────

3. If the playback sound is not clear and loud enough, adjust the Input Volume and repeat step 2.

Input Volume   ────────●────────

[Back]   [Cancel]

Beware

Sometimes audio chatting with players can lead to abuse. OnLive takes this seriously. Contact them at abuse@onlive.com.

Hot tip

Gaikai has been making progress with tablet-based play. One such tablet is the WikiPad which has an attachable gamepad controller.

Using Gaikai

Another great service which allows for the streaming of games is Gaikai. Like OnLive, it lets you play high-end games which are running on remote servers but although you can play demos on the website, the service is more geared towards allowing other companies to stream games through a browser as long as Java or Adobe Flash is installed.

You can also play Gaikai's PC games via Facebook.

Any websites which join Gaikai's network can stream PC games via embedded advertising. Among them is Walmart.com.

The Gaikai website

1   Go to Gaikai.com

2   Select Showcase at the top of the screen

3   You will see many games. Click on one

4   Select Play the Demo. Sometimes it asks for a date of birth. Use the drop-down menu to insert this

5   Gaikai will check your Java settings and, if they are fine, your game will stream. It will give you instructions on updating your Java settings if they not up-to-date

Gaikai and Facebook

Gaikai became the first company to stream blockbuster videogames via a Facebook app.

Among the games Gaikai has offered are Saints Row: The Third, Sniper: Ghost Warrior and The Witcher 2: Assassins of Kings.

You are able to play a 45-minute demo for free, after which you are directed to a payment system to buy the game if you wish:

1 Go to https://apps.facebook.com/gaikai-games/ and sign into Facebook using your email and password if you are not already signed in

2 Click on Start Playing and the Facebook permission box will appear. Gaikai will receive your basic information, email address and birthday. Click Play Game

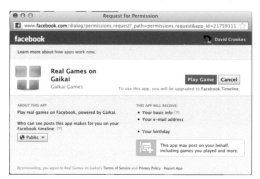

3 You can allow Gaikai to post on your behalf and access your custom friend lists. Click Allow if you want this or Skip if you do not

4 You will see a host of games. Select the one you want and click Play the Demo

5 Gaikai will check your Java settings and the game will then play. You will be shown the control method

Hot tip

Gaikai does not feature Facebook connectivity within its games so do not worry about it bombarding your status with notifications of any progress you have made.

Without Java, you will not be able to play Gaikai games. Java allows for the playing of online games as well as chat, among many other fun things so it is well worth downloading.

Installing Java for Gaikai

In order for Gaikai to work, you need to have Java installed:

 When you play a game, it will search for a Java plug-in. If it cannot detect one, it will not play the game and it will invite you to install it. Select Click here

You will be taken to the Java website in order to download the required plug-in. Choose your operating system and select the download

If you have a Mac, you will need to download Apple's own version of Java. Click on the Apple icon in the top left-hand corner of the screen and select Software Update. It will check to see if you have the latest version and prompt you to install it if not

15 Security in the cloud

Don't fall prey to danger

from the cloud.

Keep safe in the cloud

Beware

If your passwords get into the wrong hands, you are potentially allowing someone to get hold of your computing power. They may even gain the ability to lock you out of certain cloud services.

You may feel wary about having information, data and files stored in the cloud. After all, if they are being placed on someone else's server, then surely they could be accessible by a third party.

There are, however, some basic golden rules:

- Never tell anyone else your password. If someone has one of your passwords, they have the potential to access one of your cloud accounts

- It is good practice to have different passwords for different accounts. Regularly change your password

- Always remember to log out of your account when you have finished if you are on a public computer or one that you do not have the sole use of

- Do not allow your browser to remember your log in details

- When you log in, make sure you have a secure connection and that security measures are in place. The log in page URL should start with https://

- Keep your virus protection up-to-date on your computer and phone. This way you can help avoid issues such as keylogging where a piece of software monitors your keyboard activity for potential passwords

- Do not upload information of a sensitive nature such as bank details. Exercise caution

- Be wary of spam emails, particularly those which lead you to being asked for your log in details. Thieves try and trick people into divulging their information

- Only upload data to a service you trust. Hackers sometimes target cloud-based servers direct so you want to be sure they are robust enough to withstand an attack. Do your research

- Keep back-ups of important files. Even cloud services could suffer a malfunction, leading to the loss of data. It's extremely rare but you should still be on your guard

- Read the small print. Check what a service's terms and conditions entail before agreeing to them

Be safe in public Wi-Fi zones

If you access the internet via a public Wi-Fi zone (there are thousands around the world in cafes, museums, public places and so on) then you need to be extra vigilant:

Don't forget

Don't perform any sensitive tasks while you are on a public network.

- Do not allow your smartphone to access public Wi-Fi hotspots automatically. You may have signed up to a widespread service but what this means is that your phone could be logging in and out of Wi-Fi without you being aware, opening up the potential for hackers if the network is not secure

- Be especially wary of giving your personal details online when you are in a public Wi-Fi zone. Some hackers set up fake Wi-Fi hotspots or manage to penetrate the Wi-Fi connection so use public Wi-Fi for less crucial matters

- Ensure you have a good firewall on your computer and phone. This way you can block certain types of access to your device. In Windows go to Control Panel>System and Security >Windows Firewall. On a Mac, go to System Preferences >Security & Privacy>Firewall

- Encrypt files. If you are uploading files to a cloud service, consider encrypting them so that if they do fall into the wrong hands, they would be more difficult to open, thereby keeping your data much safer

● ○ ○   Security & Privacy

◀ ▶   Show All   Q

| General | FileVault | Firewall | Privacy |

◉ **Firewall: On**

The firewall is turned on and set up to prevent unauthorized applications, programs, and services from accepting incoming connections.

Stop   Click Stop to turn the firewall off.

Advanced...

🔒 Click the lock to make changes.   ?

Clearing browsers of data

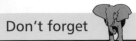

Be especially careful when using a public computer.

It is a good idea when using a public computer to ensure you have not left any trace of your browsing session, in particular passwords. We look here at how to delete them from Internet Explorer, Firefox, Chrome and Safari, using the latest browser versions.

Internet Explorer

1 Go to Tools>Internet Options

2 Select the General tab

3 Select the items you wish to delete. Click Delete

Firefox

1 Go to Firefox>Options>Security>Saved Password

2 Select Remove all

Chrome

1 Click the wrench icon

2 Select Tools>Clear browsing data

3 Tick the items you want to remove and click Clear browsing data

Safari

1 Go to Safari>Preferences

2 Select the Privacy tab

3 Click Remove all website data

S

T

W

Z